The Recruiting Game

The Recruiting Game

Toward a New System of
Intercollegiate Sports

Second Edition, Revised

John F. Rooney, Jr.

University of
Nebraska Press
Lincoln and London

The paper in this book meets the minimum requirements of American National Standard
for Information Sciences—Permanence of Paper for Printed Library Materials, ANSI
Z39.48–1984.

Library of Congress Cataloging-in-Publication Data
Rooney, John F.
   The recruiting game.
   Bibliography: p.
   Includes index.
   1. College sports—United States. 2. Athletes—
United States—Recruiting. I. Title.
GV347.R66   1987   796'.07'1173   86–19152
ISBN 0-8032-3879-7 (alk. paper)

To Ad and John, Sandy, Beth, Kate and Dan

Contents

Tables

Figures

Preface to the Second Edition

I am now more convinced than I was in 1980, when *The Recruiting Game* was first published, that big-time collegiate sports must be either purified or professionalized. The past six years have produced greater abuses to the athletes and the universities than any other period since financial aid was legalized in 1952. Newfound success at Clemson, Florida, SMU, TCU, and Illinois was closely followed by the exposure of massive cheating and NCAA probation.

In his memoirs Paul Brown, owner and coach of the Cleveland Browns, and later of the Cincinnati Bengals, described the changes in professional football after he returned to the sport in 1968: "We were getting a different type of player from the colleges and a certain percentage of them were not what I considered college material. They had been exposed to education, but not actually educated. One player of mine, for example, said, after he retired, that he wanted to return to his university to get his degree—but that it would take him three and a half years to get it. That man had already completed four years of college when he had been drafted, and I can't imagine what he had been doing during that time. His type of athlete was becoming increasingly common.''

The record of student-athlete graduation rates shows no signs of improvement. Though we lack a complete study of graduation rates for the nation's scholarship athletes, there are data on the achievement of baccalaureate degrees by the current National Football League players. Fewer than one-third of the NFL players have completed degree requirements. Considering that most of them have had a minimum of four years (many have had five) of collegiate residence and their average age is twenty-seven, the record is indeed appalling. Even more appalling is the growing attempt to rationalize the graduation problem by lauding the benefits received through exposure to a center of higher education. Growth and education by contagion is now being falsely promoted as an alternative to the real thing. Being exposed to education is, however, not the same as being educated.

This second edition provides more detail regarding the direction that purification of collegiate sport might follow. It outlines an eleven-point clean-up program. For those schools that are in the sports entertainment business, a super league based on a number of past performance variables is suggested. The new analysis of performance is derived from success-oriented variables compiled by Theodore Goudge for the 1952–83 period. New formats for conference and post-season playoffs are suggested.

All statistics on football and basketball recruitment have been updated, many through the 1985 season. New focus is also placed on ''blue chip'' recruiting, using data generated by William Sutton. An assessment of cheating and punitive action by the NCAA is featured in this edition. Also new are maps of recruiting by selected institutions, conferences, and states.

But the essential message remains unchanged. If we are to preserve the integrity of our student athletes and our universities we must change the system. Now is the time to begin!

I would like to add my thanks to graduate students Bart Mullins, Ted Goudge, and Bill Sutton, and to Susan Shaull for her assistance in typing.

Preface

The past few years have witnessed an explosion of criticism concerning big-time collegiate sports. Football and basketball have been the primary targets of the critics' wrath, though no sport has totally escaped their attention. Most of the literature has focused on the excesses involved in the hunting, recruiting, pampering and/or mistreatment of young athletes.

The cheaters have been exposed. The sordid details of the collegiate sports scene have been hashed and rehashed—to the point that anyone even marginally interested in the whole matter is no longer surprised by anything.

Why then another essay on an overworked subject? First, I believe that I have a different perspective. I am not a journalist or a disgruntled athlete. I am a part of the system, albeit from the academic side of the student-athlete myth. I have worked with and taught hundreds of athletes at a variety of sports-oriented institutions since 1963.

Second, I am greatly concerned that the recent exposés, as well as the criticisms that characterized the 1910–1950 development period of major college athletics, have failed to produce any meaningful change. The Carnegie Foundation for the Advancement of Teaching report of 1929 was followed, over the years, by a horde of critical books and articles, including a thought-provoking two-part essay by a fledgling *Sports Illustrated* editorial staff in 1956, and the onslaught culminated in 1974 in another "official" study, the American Council on Education study. The ills have been systematically and eloquently bared, but they still remain, and by most estimates the situation is getting worse.

Third, and most important, my training as a geographer equips me with unusual insights concerning the origin, development, and support of intercollegiate sport. I believe that the desire of Americans for recognition of the superiority of the place (town, state, and university) with which they are associated explains the workings of our unique intercollegiate athletic system. Place pride and the pressing need for identity, together with more leisure time and more money, have made big-time intercollegiate sport what it is today. Consequently, many of the problems related to it have a geographical cause—and a geographical solution.

My interest in the recruiting process was first aroused at my initial academic post, the University of Wyoming. In Laramie the chief source of entertainment was the Cowboy football team. Utterly amazed by the Wyomingites' fanatical attraction to the assemblage of Californians, easterners, and midwesterners who represented the university on the gridiron, I decided to investigate the process which brought them there and made them so important to the Wyoming populace.

After an exciting beginning, I moved on to UCLA, arriving there the year that Lew Alcindor did. At Westwood I became acquainted with the Wooden methods, and I began to appreciate the role that tradition, prestige, and alumni play in the recruiting game. As a bonus, I got an inside look at a truly sophisticated "brain coach" operation.

My next stop was Southern Illinois University. There, during the brief glory days of Walt "Clyde" Frazier, I received a harsh but eye-opening introduction to the devastation wrought in the colleges by the NBA hardship draft. SIU basketball had arrived with a 1967 NIT crown, but hopes for the 1968 national championship were dashed when Frazier departed early to join the New York Knicks. I spent the 1968–69 academic year as an exchange professor at the University of Exeter. It was a great escape, but most important, it introduced me to the British system of intercollegiate sport. In Britain pros are pros, amateurs are amateurs, student athletes are really students, and little, if any, aid is given to collegiate athletes. The entire experience made me wonder why our system, which was originally similar to the one in England, is now so very different.

Returning here, I assumed my present position at Oklahoma State University. It was the first university I had been associated with where the faculty talked openly and endlessly about football. The environment encouraged my growing research commitment to the geographic dimensions of sport, its origin, spread, regionalizing influences, and power to shape the character of a place. I lectured, presented papers, wrote articles and a book, *The Geography of Sport,* and even developed a heavily patronized course on the geography of sport. I met a lot of first-class student-athletes, but unfortunately I met many more who didn't care about, or weren't capable of obtaining, a baccalaureate degree.

From these experiences this essay flows. It has its source also in a deep love and affection for sport, competition, and the color, excitement, and atmosphere so often engendered by athletic events.

Perhaps this book can open the right eyes. Perhaps it can help to shape a new arena for intercollegiate sport—one characterized by honesty and fairness for all concerned.

This work would have been impossible without the assistance of my students and colleagues. Special thanks are due to a number of graduate students who have worked with me on a variety of sport geography projects. They include Mark Miller, Roger Jenkinson, Mark Rupert, Mike Johnson, Mark Okrant, Ron Pearson, Michael

Garrett, Doug McDonald, and Tom Daxon. My colleagues Richard Hecock, Bob Norris, Steve Tweedie, Bob Janiskee, and Chuck Kovacik have provided constructive critical reviews and other types of valuable assistance.

A special thanks is due Greg Mohns, who added precious hours to an overcommitted workload in order to compile a fact-filled diary of his recruiting activities. His efforts have added a great deal to this book.

I want also to thank Gayle Maxwell and Don Wade, who did most of the cartography, and Linda Allred, Jean Schwab, Connie Walker, Lisa Springer, and Dot Brabham, who typed various drafts of the manuscript. Finally, I would like to thank my wife, Sandy, for her encouragement and understanding during the development and production of this project.

The Recruiting Game

1
Introduction

I was in one car with him. A coach from another school lured him out of my car into his. Then he tore off down the highway. I was with the high school coach at the time. We started in hot pursuit after the recruit. It developed into a high-speed car chase just like you see in the movies. After about four or five minutes of running around town at eighty or ninety miles an hour, I decided that my life was more important than the recruit, so I called off the chase.[1]

This is Jerry Pettibone's description of his attempt to recruit a high school standout for the football team at Oklahoma University. Not all prospects are this elusive, but after speaking with a number of collegiate athletic recruiters, I am convinced that the events Pettibone described are relatively common occurrences. The chase for the best high school athletic talent culminates each year on "signing day." This day marks nearly four thousand official agreements that bind young men to the more than 160 NCAA Division I football schools. The day, however, seems to be especially significant in certain parts of the country. The Southeast and nearby Texas take it very seriously, as does the Big Eight territory—Oklahoma, Nebraska, and their neighbors.

The schools composing the Southeastern Conference had by tradition designated the second Saturday in December as their signing day. Signing day gets as much coverage in their areas as a major bowl game and overshadows whatever other sports happen to be in season. Regional newspapers carry complete signing data on Sunday morning, frequently accompanied by pictures and folksy interviews (figure 1).

A typical signing capsule reads something like this: "Justin's gigantic tackle, 6'5", 250, 4.9, and still growing, signed today with Ole State. At 8:30 this morning, Central Consolidated High's Bobby Don Brown signed with Cobra Beggs himself. Half the community witnessed the event." (Three photos are included to help the reader understand the enormity of the signing.) Other boys receive similar coverage, with each paper highlighting the signings of its state universities (table 1).

Joseph Durso, who compiled a book focusing on the ills of big-time intercollegiate sport, *The Sports Factory,* gave this account of the signing process at the University of Alabama.[2] Under the guidance of the late Coach Bear Bryant, Alabama had ten recruiters stationed in six states. Primed and ready for the official day, with two athletic department aircraft and three full-time pilots at his command, Bryant began his day by signing one of the hometown boys in Tuscaloosa. Within half an hour he was off to Columbus, Georgia, where he corraled All-America prospect Mike Sebastian. With Mike snared, the Bear dashed to Tampa, Florida, to sign highly prized Dewey Mitchell. According to Bryant, he only signs those who relish his personal touch: "I don't like the idea of chasing and pampering a boy and I don't do it. . . . I used to when I was younger. I'm not going to baby, beg and pet and give the boy that kind of treatment because he's sure not going to be treated that way when he gets to Alabama."[3]

Bryant's biggest recruiting opposition was a well-organized cadre of veterinarians from arch state rival Auburn. "I've never known a veterinarian who wasn't greatly concerned about Auburn football," says ex-Auburn football mentor, Shug Jordan, speak-

Figure 1. Signing day.

Table 1: National Letter Football Signees

ARKANSAS

Dick Clay, WR, 5-9, 178, Searcy.

Carlos Gatson, RB, El Dorado.

Todd Gifford, OT, 6-5, 259, Pine Bluff White Hall.

Richard Grooms, FB, 5-11, 215, Ventura, Calif., JC.

Quinn Grovey, QB, 5-11, 175, Duncan, Okla.

Albert Harris, DE, 6-2, 235, Brown Mills, N.J.

David Henson, DT-RB, 6-3, 250, Central Arkansas Christian.

Tim Horton, RB, 5-10, 175, Conway.

Steve Hudson, L, 6-5, 230, Monroe, La., Ouachita Christian.

Aaron Jackson, RB, 5-11, 185, Denison, Texas.

Greg Jackson, FB-LB, 5-11, 196, Pulaski Oak Grove.

Todd Jones, L, 6-3, 265, Little Rock Central.

Kenny Kearns, QB, 6-0, 175, Houston Memorial.

Kevin Lewis, QB, Sugarland, Texas, Clements.

Steven Marshall, LB-FB, 6-1, 210, Rivercrest.

Steve McGaha, L, 6-3, 265, Horatio.

Ken McQuay, DB, 5-11, 187, Hamburg, Ark.

Tony Ollison, DL, 6-3, 235, Malvern.

Matt Pitner, L, 6-1, 270, Houston Memorial.

Chad Rolen, 6-4, 240, Sherman, Texas.

David Schaefer, WR, 6-0, 165, Houston Northbrook.

Mike Shepherd, 6-4, 250, Monroe, La., Ouachita Christian.

Ted Shimer, LB, 6-1, 210, Bentonville.

Steve Shrigley, LB, 6-2, 235, Pulaski Oak Grove.

Charles Wade, L, 6-4, 250, Harrison.

Robert Wynn, DL, 6-2, 244, Watson Chapel.

Rodney Winston, WR/DB, 6-1, 197, Marianna, Ark.

OKLAHOMA

Tom Backes, TE, 6-6, 230, El Paso Coronado.

Nigel Clay, L, 6-4, 265, Fontana, Calif.

Phillip Collins, B, 5-9, 175, Tulsa Washington.

Robert Lee Conner, L, 6-4, 265, Mangum.

Adrian Cooper, TE, 6-3, 215, Denver South.

Scott Evans, L, 6-4, 227, Edmond.

Artie Guess, WR, 6-0, 185, OC John Marshall.

James Goode, L, 6-6, 230, Houston Yates.

Tracy Gordon, LB, 6-4, 235, Pocola.

Fred Gunter, RB, 5-8, 180, Willingboro, N.J.

Bernard Hall, QB, 6-3, 190, Detroit, Mich.

Jeff Jackson, WR, 5-11, 165, Houston Forest Brook.

Harold Jones, L, 6-4, 275, Bristow.

Darrell Kirby, L, 6-4, 235, Orlando Fla.

Terron Manning, OL, 6-1, 280, Muskogee.

Larry Medice, OT, 6-4, 275, New Orleans.

Jarrod Oliver, RB, 6-0, 215, Fort Bend, Texas.

Zarek Peters, DL, 6-4, 235, Fort Bend, Texas.

Charles Thompson, QB, 5-10, 170, Lawton.

Committed

Wayne Dixon, LB, 6-4, 207, Borger, Texas.

OKLAHOMA STATE

Mike Aboussie, LB, 6-2, 220, Arnold, Mo.

Table 1 (*continued*)

Derrick Alexander, L, 6-3, 240, Tulsa Washington.

Ricky Alsbrook, TE, 6-4, 240, Garland, Texas.

Vernon Brown, RB, 6-0, 200, Del City.

Allen Calton, LB, 6-4, 225, Fort Worth Dunbar.

Reggie Christian, L, 6-2, 230, Lewisville, Texas.

Sim Drain III, LB, 6-2, 205, Stillwater.

Joel Fry, L, 6-6, 240, Wichita North.

Fred Gaines, DB, 6-0, 185, Dallas Roosevelt.

Mike Gundy, QB, 6-0, 185, Midwest City.

Mike Hood, FB, 6-0, 218, Sulphur.

Gerald Hudson, RB, 5-11, 190, Waxahachie, Texas.

Brad King, L, 6-3, 230, Putnam City West.

Shawn Mackey, L, 6-4, 235, Marlow.

Mike Martin, OT, 6-4, 260, Morris.

Curtis Mayfield, WR, 6-2, 170, Dallas Spruce.

Terance Miller, RB, 6-0, 200, Lewisville, Texas.

Marvin Oglesby, OLB, 6-3, 215, Decatur, Ga., Towers.

Phillip Pryor, OL, 6-4, 270, Denison, Texas.

Barry Sanders, RB, 5-8, 175, Wichita, Kan., North.

Roland Scott, DL, 6-3, 205, Dallas Carter.

Chris Smith, QB, 6-2, 185, Ponca City.

Steve Tiesman, L, 6-7, 250, Bartlesville.

Terrence Tyler, L, 6-4, 235, Houston Madison.

Richard Wales, LB, 6-2, 220, Tulsa Metro Christian.

Scott Webb, L, 6-5, 240, Carroliton, Texas, Turner.

Cecil Wilson, DB, 6-1, 190, Fort Worth Dunbar.

Tim Woodford, K, 5-10, 160, Brooksfield, Fla., Hennando.

JC Transfer

Tom Caines, LB, 6-2, 225, Taft, Calif., JC.

Tyrone McClendon, DL, 6-5, 250, Taft, Calif., JC.

Jeff Patterson, DL, 6-2, 260, Northeastern A&M.

TULSA

Eric Barr, QB, 6-1, 168, Houston North Shore.

Ron Beasley, RB, 6-2, 190, Gilmer, Texas.

Dan Bitson, WR, 6-2, 185, Tulsa Washington.

Bernard Boriabi, RB, 5-11, 185, Midwest City.

Chris Brisco, DB, 5-11, 180, Wichita Kapaun–Mt. Carmel.

Frank Cassano, QB, 5-9, 170, Norristown, Pa.

John Chargois, LB, 6-3, 220, Houston Nimitz.

Rod Crawford, L, 6-3, 205, Olathe, Kans., North.

Walter Dunagin, RB, 5-11, 175, Garland, Texas.

Lee Durham, LB, 6-2, 200, Houston Waltrip.

Jerry Edgar, RB, 6-1, 190, Irving, Texas.

Chris Fancher, OT, 6-2, 230, Duncan.

Kirk Fridrich, OT/DT, 6-4, 210, Shawnee.

Kelly Harper, LB, 6-3, 205, Broken Arrow.

Pat Harper, DT, 6-1, 230, Broken Arrow.

Gill Johnson, RB, 5-7, 145, Bixby.

Craig Jones, RB/DB, 5-11, 165, Dallas Bishop Dunne.

5

Table 1: National Letter Football Signees (*continued*)

Kenneth Lee, RB, 5-11, 175, Midwest City Albert.

Kerry Miller, TE, 6-5, 215, Rochester, Minn., Mayo.

Rodney McGraw, NG, 6-2, 250, Ennis, Texas.

Marcus McVay, QB-DB, 5-11, 170, Muskogee.

Mark Oberste, TE, 6-4, 215, Sallisaw.

Billy Odell, FB, 6-0, 180, Euless, Texas.

Mickey Price, DB, 6-1, 175, Lewisville, Texas.

Joe Paul Simon, LB, 6-1, 215, Vian.

Gus Spanos, OT/DT, 6-2, 238, Pittsburgh, Pa.

Gary Treat, TE/CB, 6-3, 210, Muldrow.

Brian Wietharn, RB, Kansas City, Mo., Center.

ARKANSAS STATE

Raymond Roso, DE, 6-0, 185, Tulsa Kelley.

BAYLOR

David Frost, WR, 6-0, 180, Edmond.

SOUTHWEST MISSOURI

Harold Aldridge, DB, 6-2, 180, Muskogee.

Brian Eddy, L, 6-3, 235, Tulsa East Central.

TEXAS

Paul Behrman, DB, 6-0, 185, Norman.

WICHITA STATE

Smiley Elmore Jr., RB, 5-11, 190, Tulsa Kelley.

Jarod Mendenhall, 6-2, 185, Enid.

NON-DIVISION I

Central Missouri—Michael Mornes, B, 5-9, 185, Tulsa Rogers.

Pittsburg State—John Jackson, B, 5-9, 160, Tulsa Rogers; Daryl Wren, B, 6-3, 170, Tulsa Rogers.

Tennessee-Martin—Willie Ramsey, L, 6-2, 255, Tulsa Memorial.

SOURCE: *Tulsa World*, February 1985.

ing of the recruitment of young athletes in Alabama and surrounding states.[4]

The scene is similar in Oklahoma and Texas. Lists of who signed where, and filmed interviews with the prize athletes, parents, and coaches are carried by local TV sports shows. The landing of a superstar merits front-page treatment, while the remainder of the sports section is devoted to the details. Basketball, hockey, wrestling, and swimming—the sports in season—must take a back seat to the football signing news. The signing of some of America's most widely coveted athletes has been the focus of numerous popular magazine articles. In fact, the recuitment of potential superstars has been given book-length coverage.[5] Dan Jenkins's "Pursuit of a Big Blue-Chipper" was a colorful probe of collegiate recruitment and is a reasonably accurate account of what a top prospect still endures. Jenkins described the typical blue-chipper as "big, tough, intelligent, unselfish, a leader. And fast? He runs the 100 in 9.4—uphill. Man that's a 4.4 forty. He's got it all, which is why Ara, Bear, and Darrell and the Detroit Tigers and the Boston Celtics and the Mogan Guaranty Trust have all been trying to sign him up since he was in the fourth grade."[6]

The object of Jenkins's attention was Jack Mildren, who gained fame as the first wishbone quarterback at the University of Oklahoma. Mildren, from Cooper High School in Abilene, Texas, was like many other potential football stars: he had only a vague notion of where he wanted to go. He hoped to stay close to home, but in football-rich Texas, Oklahoma, and Arkansas, that desire still provided a wide range of choice.

Jack and his parents planned to visit the universities on his "possible" list during the summer before his senior year. Word of his arrival always seemed to precede him, resulting in a guided tour instead of a low-key personal look. Each university he visited believed that it had a good chance of recruiting Mildren.

Oklahoma was the first to enter the fray. Barry Switzer, the present OU mentor, spent many hours with Mildren and his family. He got the jump on the Southwest Conference schools, whose rules precluded contact until after a senior had completed his final game.

After Cooper High's final game the quest began in earnest. Telegrams flowed in. Mildren was pestered with phone calls. Everyone wanted to arrange an appointment. From Darrel Royal: "Where do we stand, Jack? Is Texas in this? If you come to our place you must know that your opportunities for success will be greater than they would be if you went anywhere else. If you plan to live in Texas you ought to attend the University. It's that simple." Royal went on to say, "You're a competitor, Jack. Come to our place, roll up your sleeves, and show 'em who's best. The challenge is there. The question is whether you're man enough to meet it."[7] Along with the numerous recruiting pitches from coaches, Jack received many calls from professional players and famous alumni. Texas All-Americans and All-Pros put in a word for their institutions.

A great many people spent their money and time vying for the privilege of signing Jack Mildren to a national letter of intent. He was hosted by former star athletes, celebrities, and beauty queens. His ultimate decision to attend the University of Oklahoma was very difficult. There was such a wide range of choices and so many variables were involved. It was a monumental task, and though his dilemma was somewhat more extreme than that of the typical schoolboy athlete, it nonetheless illustrates the difficulties involved in the decision-making process.

The Mildren story is not an isolated incident. It is representative of what happens to the best prospects, but by Mildren's own wish, his possible choices were confined to a few states. The recruiting saga of Jimmy Cefalo, the recent Penn State star who played with the Miami Dolphins, better epitomizes the national scope of the collegiate recruiting game.[8] Cefalo was a high school All-American from Pittston, Pennsylvania, sought by nearly every big-name school in the country.

Cefalo said his recruitment was an outstanding learning experience. "Some recruiters showed me a realistic college life, while others presented a rose-colored spectacle." One university wanted to show him college life as it is. The coach asked him to talk to the students — "Use your weekend visit to learn as much as you can about our school." Jim thought that was a good idea; in contrast, "At an Atlantic Coast Conference college I was shown only what the recruiters wanted me to see."

Cefalo's high school was overwhelmed by eager recruiters. Despite this he was unsure of his potential as a major college player. He became skeptical, believing that recruiters would say whatever they thought he wanted to hear. He encountered a great deal of insincerity—from a recruiter at a Big Eight school, "You should visit our college because you like to eat steak and our state raises milk-fed cows." He began to feel that he was a commodity. His experience with one footloose coach, who switched jobs during the year that Jimmy was being pursued, served to reinforce that belief. He forgot that he had met Cefalo before, making the same pitch for two different universities: "Jimmy, this university is the best for you. You'll play varsity football early. You'll be able to follow the major of your choice. I think you'll be doing what's best if you sign with us."

Cefalo's final decision was based on the low-pressure approach employed by Penn State and Joe Paterno. He was encouraged to investigate all segments of college life. No promises were made. He noted that other football players and students lauded Paterno. "I knew he was interested in my life and my personality; we talked about a variety of things, rarely football."

A number of recruiting sagas are recounted by Durso and also by Jim Benagh in his *Making It to #1*.[9] Durso covers the quest for Butch Lee, of DeWitt Clinton High School in New York City, who went on to lead Marquette to the NCAA basketball title.[10] Lee was the most heavily recruited guard in the country. His services were sought by over two hundred schools. Durso described the two Marquette recruiters, Rick Majerus and Jack Burke, as a "team not unlike a pair of homicide detectives grilling a suspect. Majerus would be the heavy, planting the ideas in the suspect's head. Burke would be the nice guy, keeping things on an even keel in case the suspect worried too much about Majerus' tough guy approach."[11] The strategy worked as Lee selected Marquette over Duke, Maryland, Penn, and Detroit.

Benagh goes into great detail in describing the recruitment of Rich Allocco, a blue-chip running back from New Jersey.[12] Lured by 265 schools, Allocco finally narrowed his choices to Michigan, Ohio State, Nebraska, Penn State, and Notre Dame, the eventual winner. Benagh discusses each of Allocco's campus visits as well as the bird-dogging that the prospect experienced at his New Jersey home. The account focuses on the different strategies employed in attempting to land his services and points out the almost unbelievable ends to which our major institutions will go to corral a blue-chipper. Robert Six, president of Continental Airlines, said that if Allocco attended the University of Colorado, the airline would be at his service.[13] Rice and Nebraska both catered to his Catholicism, Nebraska utilizing a woman counselor who happened to be a former nun.[14] Allocco also received letters from governors, mayors, corporation heads, college presidents, and a variety of influential alumni. The recruiting process involved the time, money, and effort of many people, and ultimately, of course, only one institution would receive any sort of return on its investment.

Willie Morris, in *The Courting of Marcus Dupree*, devotes over 400 pages to the recruitment of one high school stalwart.[15] He recounts his senior season and the dizzier adventures that followed before Dupree's decision to sign with Oklahoma. The stress endured over the course of recruiting was clearly related to the ultimate failure that Marcus experienced. Following a sensational freshmen debut, he was publicly criticized by Coach Barry Switzer and dropped out of the university in the middle of his sophomore season.

The NCAA recently imposed a 33 percent reduction in the number of football scholarships. That still calculates to over four thousand annual signings by our major colleges, and twice as many boys receive scholarships from the so-called small schools. As was apparent in the cases of Mildren, Cefalo, and the others, the competition for the blue-chippers is unbelievably fierce. Even the journeymen players are difficult to find and recruit, particularly when one considers the fact that there are nearly a half-million juniors and seniors playing high school football.

A successful athletic program is dependent on the effective recruiting of both players and coaches. Good recruiting does not guarantee a good team, but without it there is no hope. In the words of Don Canham, athletic director at the University of Michigan: "Recruiting is a justified pursuit. . . . It's a necessary evil. For instance, if we did not recruit and have great football teams [at Michigan], we wouldn't have anything going. We wouldn't have any money. It's absolutely essential in our system in amateur athletics today."[16] In this era of subsidized athletes, the name of the game is winning, and winning big is even better.

2
The Origin
and Growth of
Intercollegiate Athletics

The recruiting game has not always been the fierce pursuit it is today. Shopping for collegiate players in a national, and in some cases international, athletic marketplace is an outgrowth of an evolutionary process that began over one hundred years ago. American intercollegiate sport has undergone profound change over the past century. Our colleges and universities now serve different purposes and a much wider clientele. Big-time sport is the most visible side effect of this metamorphosis. Among gentlemen, prior to 1820, there was a general contempt for physical prowess. It was a contempt in keeping with prevailing English attitudes toward frivolity, tied closely to the Puritan ethic. The majority of college graduates were entering the ministry, hence the need for intellectual growth took precedence over physical education.

The intercollegiate sport breakthrough occurred between 1820 and 1852. Harvard was the innovator, establishing both intramural and interclass athletic programs for its student body. The Harvard sports day, Bloody Monday, soon became famous throughout the Northeast. Sports days sprang forth at other eastern universities, paving the way for intercollegiate competition.

The first intercollegiate contest was an eight-oared barge race held on Lake Winnipesaukee in New Hampshire. The year was 1852, and Harvard and Yale were the competing colleges. From that time until 1880 there was a slow but steady growth in both intramural and intercollegiate competition, though it was confined mostly to the Northeast. By 1860 intercollegiate baseball competition was well established, with over a dozen schools fielding teams. Intramural soccer was also popular.

Intercollegiate football (soccer) began as an offshoot of a heated baseball rivalry between Princeton and Rutgers. The spring baseball game of 1869 was pivotal. Princeton defeated Rutgers in that contest, prompting the losers' Varsity Football Club to issue a challenge. That challenge resulted in the game that is now cited as the first American intercollegiate football match. From 1869 to 1877, intercollegiate football games resembling soccer were played intermittently. Local rules prevailed, meaning that size of field, number of players, and time limits were negotiable. Columbia, CCNY, Harvard, Haverford, New York University, the University of Pennsylvania, and Yale were the leaders in the burgeoning sports movement.

Modifications of American soccer began almost immediately following the first intercollegiate game. Although the documentation of these changes is sketchy, it is known that Harvard and Yale played leadership roles. Harvard, influenced by McGill, a Canadian university, adopted rugby union football rules in 1874.

It was a period of much bickering. Some schools preferred soccer; others leaned toward rugby union. The dispute was settled at a convention called in 1876, with the carrying game (rugby) winning over the kicking game (soccer). Following the convention, an intercollegiate football association dedicated to the game of rugby union was established. The rules governing rugby union were changed annually, and as a result the uniquely American game of football gradually emerged.

By 1880, a number of competitive frameworks had been organized. Leagues and conferences linked schools together and promoted competition in track, rowing, and baseball.

During this early period of intercollegiate athletic expansion, team management was in the hands of the undergraduate student body. The coaches were either members of the faculty or students. In fact, the faculty and students coached and competed together, as eligibility rules were nonexistent. Most sport historians date the takeoff of intercollegiate sports from around 1880. The ensuing decade marked the beginning of an ominous movement. Paid coaches, gate receipts, trainers, and alumni solicitation and control all came into being. Strangely, the faculty at most universities remained aloof. Perhaps they were unaware of the takeover, for they sat idly by while their rights to govern were stripped away. By 1887 most universities had established central committees composed of alumni, paid coaches, students, and a sprinkling of faculty members for the purpose of controlling their athletic programs.

I believe that the decision to adopt serious intercollegiate athletic programs was in large part prompted by what might be termed a "glory of the place," or place-boosting, philosophy, combined with the growing commercial drive that in general characterized American society. Victory in athletic competition represented a concrete expression of superiority: "My place is a grand place; my place is better than your place." Thus the "team" became a vehicle of community and school pride. Old grads, students, and the local residents wanted to call attention to their university and their place, and they were willing to pay whatever price was necessary to insure success. It was this same "glory of the town" ideal that transformed baseball from a purely amateur gentlemen's game into a full-fledged professional sport. That change occurred between 1850 and 1870 and set the stage for the commercial development of intercollegiate football.

The New York Knickerbockers, 1840s version, are recognized as the first organized baseball team in America.[1] During those early years the Knickerbocker brand of baseball was definitely an aristocratic gentlemen's game, just as early collegiate athletics were in the sport for sport's sake mold. The Knickerbockers were founded as a social club; forty to fifty gentlemen met to play baseball in much the same way that groups now organize as country clubs for the purpose of playing golf and tennis. The early baseball clubs were popular, class-oriented social organizations.

Early baseball emphasized sportsmanship and socializing. Most of the participants were men of position, and a little wealth didn't hurt one's chances for making the team. After the Civil War, a conflict which exposed the rudiments of baseball to soldiers from both sides, the game began to diffuse vigorously. Albert B. Hart, writing in 1890, attributed the development of public interest in a variety of field sports to the contacts resulting from the Civil War.[2] Baseball was a major beneficiary, spreading geographically and also breaking through and across class lines. In many communities the central objective moved from sport for sport's sake to winning for the glory of the town. Thus the role of sport in the elusive relationship that exists between people and their respective places was strengthened.

American pride in place, an outgrowth of the democratic booster enthusiasm for life, has helped to shape the locational pattern of present-day sport, particularly its unique intercollegiate structure. The establishment, and eventual success, of a great many American communities and institutions of higher learning stemmed from boosterism. The impulse to boost one's place, and the pride in community, state, region, and country which underlies the impulse, is simply the American way.[3] This preoccupation with projecting a winning image led quite naturally to athletic recruiting. It was a logical and predictable development in a society imbued with the frontier spirit, a booster mentality, and competition on all fronts.

For baseball the transition from amateur to professional status went something like this. A team from one town, thinking that a team from another town might be too tough to beat, sought out and paid a few of the most talented players in their area to play for them. Not to be outdone, rival communities engaged in the same practice. In some cases players would move from town to town, representing a different team each weekend. Some of the best players jumped clubs with reckless abandon, often competing against

15

the same team that they had played for the week before. The desire of so many towns to field a winning team eventually led to the professionalization of baseball.

Winning was important because it brought prestige to the community. A contemporary newspaper account of an 1867 intersectional contest pitting the Forest City Club of Rockford, Illinois, against the touring Washington Nationals accurately conveys the relationship between winning and the "glory of the town" ethos: "Touring the West and defeating the top clubs of that region, the Nationals crushed western pride until a Cinderella team, the Forest City Club of Rockford, defeated the Nationals, 29 to 23, at Chicago's Dexter Park. Out of pride-filled hearts, the Rockford citizenry honored its heroes with watches, gold pins, and other gifts. Nor did local pride end there, for the town celebrated for a week."[4]

It appears that the universities learned from the recruiting and compensation practices that the town baseball club sponsors had pioneered. Recruitment of college athletes began during the 1880s, about ten years after the professional baseball movement. College football had begun the transition from an extracurricular recreational activity to a highly commercialized sport form. Prior to 1900 compensation usually amounted to some type of employment, lodging, meals, and other kinds of favors. It was primarily funded by fraternities and alumni. Only the best althletes were subsidized and scholarship offers were commonly vague. The typical offer stated that the athlete would be well cared for if he came to the university.[5]

The system was extremely flexible.[6] Loosely monitored, it produced the tramp athlete and the ringer, and resulted in a situation similar to that which had occurred during the creeping commercialism era of baseball. Some boys wore the colors of five or six different schools during their intercollegiate athletic careers. At the extreme were those who played for different universities on alternate weekends, or for a college team on Saturday and a professional team on Sunday.

Throughout these early days the bulk of the recruiting was done by mail. The major participants in the recruiting game, aside from the players and college coaches, were alumni and high school mentors. Since most of the major universities had minute enrollments, the dean of admissions became a very powerful individual. He controlled who got in and how much an athlete would receive for his services.

Football was the first intercollegiate sport to bloom as a public entertainment. Baseball, which had developed the American appetite for sports entertainment, was a summer game. College football simply extended the time frame, and with the advent of bowl games, it satisfied spectator needs through New Year's Day. By the 1920s the game had swept most of the nation. As football began to challenge professional baseball for the sporting dollar and fan loyalty, its movement from the Northeast was hastened by the pilfering of coaches from the established schools. It was musical chairs for coaches in those days too. Walter Camp, Fielding Yost, and Gil Dobie moved to the West Coast, while John Heisman, Mike Donahue, and Daniel McGugin Brought the game to the South, and Amos Alonzo Stagg and Frank Cavanaugh left the East Coast in favor of the Midwest.

The rate of intercollegiate football diffusion gained momentum after World War I, and was accompanied by the intensification of recruiting. Proven coaches and promising high school players were widely sought. Eastern coaches like Howard Jones, Glenn "Pop" Warner, and Andy Smith brought their brand of football to the Pacific Coast. The South emerged as a formidable football region, led by Alabama, Georgia Tech, and Tennessee. Small schools like Notre Dame, Centre College, and Texas A & M rocketed to overnight fame. Knute Rockne, Bernie Bierman, Bob Zuppke, Lynn "Pappy" Waldorf, and Bob Neyland emerged as the folk heroes of their day.

The rise of Centre College between 1917 and 1921 is indicative of how low-key and disorganized recruiting was during this period. This obscure little school in Danville, Kentucky, reached its peak in 1921 when the Praying Colonels handed Harvard its first defeat in five seasons. Many of Centre's key performers had accompanied Chief Myers, their high school coach at North Side

High in Fort Worth, Texas, when he assumed the football reins at the college. In the words of Bo McMillin, the team's All-America quarterback: "Chief was appointed head football coach at Centre, and all the North Side boys who could meet the entrance requirements followed him there."[7]

The ascension of collegiate football stimulated a boom in stadium construction. Most of the big-name schools felt compelled to erect a colossal structure to house their gridiron show. Because the majority of the colleges were located in small towns, the gigantic buildings could serve no other purpose. The schools built facilities with borrowed funds, planning to pay them off with gate receipts. Since attendance was markedly influenced by the quality of play, the stadium debt provided a powerful motive to field a successful team. With so many universities seeking the same goals, severe competition for the available talent resulted. The modern era of high-pressure recruiting had begun.

Opposition to the recruitment and subsidization of college players was widespread but ineffective. The NCAA officially condemned recruiting, as did the powerful and trend-setting Big Nine (now the Big Ten) Conference. College officials were constantly on the anti-commercialism soapbox, and few years passed without published statements of that position.[8] Still, despite the reasoned criticism, the public and alumni had their way. Recruiting and subsidization relentlessly grew.

The 1920s saw numerous violations of the amateur athletic code, prompting even more call for reform. Finally the Carnegie Foundation for the Advancement of Teaching answered them by funding a thorough study of American college athletics. Under the directorship of Howard Savage the results were published in 1929:

Before, say, 1917, recruiting appears to have been conducted by enthusiastic undergraduates and by athletes themselves more generally than it is today, except at a few institutions where fraternities have not yet outgrown such practices. The subsidizing that accompanied recruiting under these auspices was comparatively ineffectual and certainly crude. Since those days, a more businesslike procedure has been developed by older persons on the basis of experience in previous years and in the field of commerce. About 1919, there began to spread through the East and South and along the Pacific Coast a contagion of ready assistance to promising athletes, which was initiated and coordinated mainly by older hands. The result is that today, notwithstanding many statements to the contrary, the colleges and universities of the United States are confronted with acute problems of recruiting and subsidizing, especially with respect to intercollegiate football.[9]

Recruiting and subsidizing were in violation of the amateur code. Furthermore, they brought students to college campuses for the wrong reasons. In an attempt to focus on the cause of these illegal activities, Savage went on to say:

The bearing of subsidizing upon the amateur status comes down at last to a question of motive. No matter what the source of the subsidy, if the reason behind it can be accurately determined, the status of the athlete becomes at once clear. Given a skilled fullback who is receiving from a head football coach $100 a month, if it can be proved that the motive for this provision concerns not at all the ability or prominence of the athlete, then the athlete is not thereby professionalized, whatever be the presumptions to the contrary. But in such a case, the mere assertion of innocence is not to be taken as proof. On the other hand, any favor, however small, that tends to assist an athlete financially, if it is done because he is an athlete, marks the beginning of professionalism. There is no valid reason why even the most worthy athlete should receive any consideration, favor, assistance, or attention that is not available, upon the same terms and with the same readiness, to the general body of undergraduates. Nor is it easy to see how the sincere amateur could expect such special consideration or advantage.[10]

The Carnegie Foundation concluded that over 30 percent of the recruiting was handled by alumni and about 10 percent by administrative, academic, or executive officers of the university. Most of the rest was in the hands of athletic departments. The report also concluded that only *one in seven* athletes was being subsidized.

A return to purely amateur sport was strongly recommended, but the colleges' lust for national recognition through football was a powerful stumbling block to the reform movement. The colleges were not ready to clean house despite pleas from numerous influential sources. Fritz Crisler, then the head football coach at Princeton, speaking in 1937, stated the need for amateurism: "Your athletic ability is too sacred to sell. If you would gain the respect of your fellow man don't sell or bargain it."[11]

One man stood out as an implacable foe of overemphasis. "Robert Maynard Hutchins continued his assault on the sporting mania within university walls and did much to persuade the great institutions that athletic preeminence was not vital to a true university. He preached a doctrine of de-emphasis, claiming that the emphasis on athletics and social life that infects all colleges and universities has done more than most things to confuse these institutions and to debase higher learning in America. The University of Chicago dropped football after the 1939 season."[12]

Recruiting decreased, but only as a result of the Depression, after which World War II produced a forced de-emphasis. In fact, many universities dropped football for two or three seasons during the war. The military service training programs, particularly the air force preflight training and the navy V-5 and V-12 programs, kept college football alive during the war. Most of the great players were at the service academies or in naval, air force, or marine training programs, their scholarships courtesy of the federal government.

National rankings took on a strange appearance during the war. Notre Dame, Army, and Navy were still near the top, but so were the V-5 and V-12 centers, Tulsa, Colorado College, Georgetown, Southwestern Louisiana, Southwest Texas, and Rochester.

The immediate postwar years were dominated by returning military veterans. Recruiting for their services was intense and set the stage for what now exists.

Pressures to recruit were boosted by the new rules governing substitution. Prior to World War II football had been an eleven-man game. The NCAA rules committee legalized substitution in 1941 to compensate for the loss of quality players to the war effort. Substitution was liberalized further in 1946 and again in 1949, thereby increasing the number of athletes necessary to field a quality team. Spiraling costs led to a short-lived elimination of full-scale two-platoon football in 1953.

There were some notable attempts to stem the mounting charge toward open athletic subsidies and national recruiting. Everett Case, president of Colgate University, speaking in 1947, stated that subsidization of college football players creates a vicious circle:

Where is the glory in a Colgate victory won by men not picked and developed from the regular student body but offered special financial inducements to "represent" you? What would you think of your college if we used funds entrusted to us for educational purposes to go out and hire a football team?

Actually, this easy way out isn't even smart. Subsidization creates a vicious circle. What we do, our conpetitors have the right to do, and greater resources to do it with. Then how can subsidization, if generally practiced, assure victory for any given team?[13]

In 1948, University of Missouri athletic director and head football coach Don Faurot complained bitterly about the recruitment of Missouri high-schoolers. He asked the NCAA to stop out-of-state schools—Arkansas, Kentucky, Tulane, Mississippi State, Alabama, and Kansas among them—from offering aid to "his" Missouri boys. Citing expense-paid trips to out-of-state campuses (perfectly legal today) and player tryouts as examples of unethical practices, he threatened to bolt the NCAA so that Missouri could meet the competition.[14]

Partially in response to the Missouri allegations, Coach Paul "Bear" Bryant of the University of Kentucky decided in 1951 to phase out the recruitment of nonstate athletes.[15] Out-of-state football scholarships would be limited to five and would ultimately be eliminated altogether. The growing desire to restrain national recruiting was evident in a 1956 *Sports Illustrated* survey of college administrators and football coaches. One of the nine "survival" recommendations designed to head off the college football crisis addressed the problem: "A fixed percentage of athletic scholarships—we suggest 75%—should be reserved only for boys in the conference territory of the college or university and its environ."[16]

By then the NCAA had established a new set of national standards. Financial aid to collegiate athletes was legalized in 1952. Athletic scholarships and grants-in-aid were formalized and given official status. Any institution could recruit and subsidize athletes from any area of the country. Thus what had once been deemed out-and-out professionalism, buying and selling athletic talent on the open market, gradually, and without any real justification, became legitimate. The numerous and often eloquent pleas for reason had gone unheeded. In fact, the decision to move to a sanctioned aid system occurred just one year after Sen. J. William Fulbright's now famous "morality" speech. Fulbright saw the intercollegiate athletic scene as symptomatic of general societal malaise:

Let us consider what has developed in our colleges, where the characters of our young men and women are being molded. Our colleges, under extreme pressure from the alumni, have become so intent upon winning games that they use any means to attain their ends.

They hire players who are not bona fide students and thus make a mockery, a farce, of the whole concept of amateur sport for the health and entertainment of our young men. They corrupt not only the hired players, but also the entire student body who learn from their elders the cynical, immoral doctrine that one must win at all costs.[17]

The search for quality schoolboy athletes has continued to intensify. The substitution rule that in 1952 forced a return to single-platoon football and thereby relieved some of the recruiting pressure didn't last long. It was soon replaced by a more liberal substitution rule which in turn gave way to free substitution and the player specialization that now exists. Kids aren't just football players any more; they are wide receivers, cornerbacks, linebackers, kickers, or one of several other narrowly defined positions. And frequently they are trained for a particular position from a very early age.

Recruiting has become more sophisticated with each passing year. Nearly every major institution has come to believe that the entire nation is its source region for the truly great prospects, and because the athletes themselves are an extremely heterogeneous group, many schools now have coaching staffs with diverse geographical and ethnic backgrounds. Ever-increasing pressures to win, combined with limitations on the number of scholarships that can be awarded, have made recruiting both more important and more difficult than ever before.

3
The
Nuts and Bolts
of Recruiting

How does a university proceed with the business of recruiting athletes? There are certain common denominators which apply to all of the major institutions and, on a smaller scale, to most of the schools that field athletic teams.

The typical university goes to great lengths to monitor the development of athletes in its own region. Questionnaires are systematically circulated to all state high schools and to many of those located in surrounding states (figure 2). The questionnaires are usually addressed to the high school coaches and seek data on high school juniors. They are designed to assemble information on a player's position, size, and speed. Each coach is asked to rank the players from his high school. Frequently the coach will also volunteer his opinions on the potential of his young stalwarts for big-time football, basketball, or other sport. At this early stage of recruiting, the high school coach's track record for supplying reliable information is extremely critical.

Each university develops a network of dependable coaches, usually including a significant number from outside the local area.

TOP PROSPECTS IN ORDER OF ABILITY — _____ SCHOOL YEAR

NAME	POS.	HT.	WT.	40 YD. SPEED	HOME ADDRESS AND PHONE
Coach's name:			Phone:		
School:			Town:		

Figure 2. Football prospect survey.

We would appreciate your supplying us with the following information which will be added to your file. Our coach who recruits in your area will be able to contact you again after the completion of your season. Thank you.

NAME _____ NICKNAME _____
(Last)   (First)   (Middle)

ADDRESS _____ HOME PHONE _____
(Number)   (Street)   (Area Code)   (Number)

CITY _____ STATE _____ ZIP CODE _____

HIGH SCHOOL/JUCO _____ YEAR GRAD: _____ SCHOOL PHONE _____
(Area Code)   (Number)

PARENTS NAME _____ CHURCH PREFERENCE _____

PARENTS' ALMA MATER _____ PARENT'S OCCUPATION _____

YOUR BIRTH DATE _____ HT. _____ WT. _____ SPEED 40 YDS. _____ JERSEY NO. _____
(Month)   (Day)   (Year)

POSITION PLAYED — Off. _____ Def. _____ HIGH SCHOOL COACH'S NAME _____ COACH'S HOME PHONE _____

HIGH SCHOOL PRINCIPAL'S NAME: _____ PHONE: _____

HONORS RECEIVED _____

HIGH SCHOOL COUNSELOR'S NAME _____ YOUR PREFERRED COURSE OF STUDY _____

ACT SCORE _____ SAT SCORE _____ RANK IN CLASS _____ G.P.A. _____

FAMILY AND FRIENDS WHO HAVE ATTENDED OKLA. STATE _____

WHAT WOULD YOU LIKE TO DO FOLLOWING COLLEGE GRADUATION? _____

Figure 3. Detailed prospect data.

25

The list of coaches is built up over the years as athletes from various places come to the university's attention. If a high school coach believes that he has a prospect capable of making it at the university requesting information, he will often volunteer game films and additional statistics on the prospect.

Most schools also send a second, more detailed questionnaire directly to the prospect (figure 3). The athletes who will receive the second questionnaire are chosen from the high school all-state and All-America listings. These sources of information are supplemented by subscriptions to major metropolitan newspapers in areas noted for quality high school football. Regional and national recruiting services, which frequently provide no more than a compilation of available athletes broken down by height, weight, speed, and position, also help to fill out the blue-chip lists. (These services are particularly important for basketball, a sport in which just one or two outstanding recruits can make the difference.) In addition, a number of athletic flesh peddlers roam the metropolitan ghettos, feeding information (for a price) to the universities that want it.

A major football school will probably gather data on a minimum of 2,000 high school and junior college athletes each year. Of that number a few will be superstars who are already at the top of everyone's "most wanted list"; the rest must be measured and evaluated by the coaching staff. This sifting process is accomplished through the analysis of game films (often taking thousands of man-hours) and telephone conversations with high school coaches. Following many months of tedious effort, the number of athletes to be pursued is reduced to a few hundred. Then the personal contact period begins in earnest.

The head football coach and the recruiting coordinator, usually one of the assistant coaches, divide up the state and other important supply areas. The assistant coaches are each allocated a territory. After working the same region for a number of years, the assistant coach develops a rapport with that region's alumni and high school coaches. These contacts are so important that an assistant who moves on to a new school is likely to be assigned to his old recruiting area. In fact, regional recruiting contacts contribute significantly to the job switching that epitomizes the profession. Good recruiters are always in demand.

With the burgeoning of national recruiting it is now common for the recruiting coordinator and some of the coaches to make trips to several of the most fertile supply areas. As many as ten or fifteen cities may be designated for the recruiting blitz. Potentially helpful alumni or high school coaches in the area will be notified of the impending visit and asked to line up game films on the area's top prospects. If this is not possible, the university coach who is recruiting the area will do it himself. After a week or two, depending upon the size of the city, a group of five to ten prospects will be identified and contacted.

The coach will try to observe each player under consideration in an actual game. If a prospect is still deemed worthwhile, the coach will visit with him, his parents, appropriate high school officials, and anyone else who might help to convince the lad to attend the school in question. If all goes well, he will then be invited to the campus for a forty-eight-hour visit. What happens on campus in the course of the visit varies from campus to campus. In some cases the athlete may be asked to sign a letter of intent; in others, he is simply asked to look around and investigate the university on his own. He may be lavishly entertained, wooed by the coeds, hustled by famous alumni, or merely taken out to dinner by one of the assistant coaches. The visit also includes an audience with the head coach and a chance to talk to a faculty member in the prospect's anticipated major. Unfortunately, the faculty who help with athletic recruiting are apt to be, in effect, salesmen working for the glory of the athletic department and their appraisal of the university often tends to be as rosy and biased as that of the coaching staff.

Once a school places an athlete on its wanted list, the athletic establishment makes a point of staying in touch with him. NCAA rules now limit recruiters to three home visits. Helpful alumni in the boy's community are also asked to do their part. This usually translates into maintaining his interest in the university, but they may also be asked to help keep tabs on the competition.

Recruiting Controls

There are controls on every phase of the recruiting game. Major college recruiting is administered by the National Collegiate Athletic Association. In addition, the NCAA has responsibility for a host of smaller schools. The National Association of Intercollegiate Athletics is the supervisory agent for another group of small-budget institutions. Violations of the code applying to athletic recruitment must first be brought to the attention of the NCAA or NAIA before an investigation can be authorized.

Some of the basic rules that govern the "game" are worth citing here. They deal with the identification and description of the student-athlete, the role of alumni or friends of the university, gifts to potential student athletes, transportation, and regulations concerning "tryouts," talent scouts, and sports camps. According to the NCAA:

[Definition of An Athlete.] A "student-athlete" is a student whose matriculation was solicited by a member of the athletic staff or other representative of athletic interests with a view toward the student's ultimate participation in the intercollegiate athletic program. Any other student becomes a "student-athlete" only when he reports for an intercollegiate squad which is under the jurisdiction of the department of intercollegiate athletics. A student is not deemed a "student-athlete" solely because of his prior participation in high school athletics.

[Alumni Involvement.] If an institution's staff member requests an alumnus or other friend of the institution to recruit a particular prospect, or has knowledge that an alumnus or friend is recruiting the prospect, then said alumnus or friend becomes a "representative of athletic interests" of that institution. Once a person is identified as a representative, it is presumed he retains that identity.

[Gifts.] An institution's staff member or any other representative of an institution's athletic interests shall not, during recruitment of an individual and prior to the individual's enrollment at the institution, be involved, directly or indirectly, in making arrangements for or giving or

28

offering to give financial aid or other benefits to the prospective student-athlete, his relatives or friends, other than expressly permitted by governing legislation of this Association. This prohibition shall apply regardless of whether similar financial aid, benefits or arrangements are available to prospective students in general, their relatives or friends. Specifically prohibited financial aid, benefits and arrangements include, but are not limited to: arrangement of employment of the relatives of a prospective student-athlete; gift of clothing or equipment; the cosigning of loans; provision of loans to the relatives or friends of a prospective student-athlete; cash or like items; any tangible items including merchandise, free or reduced-cost services or rental or purchases of any type, and free or reduced-cost housing. The arrangement of employment for, and the acceptance of loans from a regular lending agency (based upon a regular repayment schedule) by the prospective student-athlete shall be permitted.

[Contacts.] No more than three such contacts per prospective student-athlete, which shall include contacts with his relative or legal guardian, shall be permitted by any single institution.

Bona fide alumni organizations of an institution may sponsor luncheons, teas or dinners at which prospective students (athletes and non-athletes) of that locale are guests.

[Tryouts.] No member institution shall, on its campus or elsewhere, conduct or have conducted in its behalf any athletic practice, tryout or test at which one or more prospective student-athletes reveal, demonstrate or display their abilities in any phase of any sport.

[Transportation, Visitations and Entertainment.] A member institution may finance one and only one visit to its campus for a given prospective student-athlete. Such visit shall not exceed forty-eight hours. Only actual round-trip transportation costs by direct route between the student's home and the institution's campus may be paid. If commercial air transportation is used, the fare may not exceed tourist.

[Talent Scouts.] An institution shall not pay any costs incurred by an athletic talent scout or a representative of its athletic interests in studying or recruiting prospective student-athletes. An institution may not place

any such person on a fee or honorarium basis and thereby claim him as a staff member entitled to expense money.

[Specialized Sports Camps, Coaching Schools and Clinics.] In operating a specialized sports camp, coaching school or sports clinic, a member institution, members of its staff or representatives of its athletic interests shall not employ or give free or reduced admission privileges to a high school or junior college athletic award winner.[1]

Enforcement of the rules is an impossible task. There is simply no way to maintain surveillance of over 700 active institutional members. The NCAA currently employs twenty men (double the 1980 force) in the enforcement department to police all recruiting activities as well as to monitor the in-house care and feeding of athletes! With such a small investigative force, illicit behavior has a high probability of success.

Variations in Recruiting

OHIO STATE

Appreciation of the sophisticated and competitive nature of collegiate athletic recruiting can be sharpened by a closer look at the operations of a few institutions. Robert Vare has done an excellent job of describing the Ohio State recruiting setup in his recent book, *Buckeye*.[2] The Ohio State system was administered by Woody Hayes (prior to being fired for his 1978 Gator Bowl antics) with ample help from a 300-member alumni group, known as the Athletic Committee, whose task it is to scout potential Buckeyes throughout Ohio and other prime football supply centers.

Each of the 300 committeemen plays a part in the sifting and recruiting process that draws prospects for the Ohio State football team. Most of the committeemen are donors to the athletic department and enthusiastic participants in athletic department functions. According to Vare some are active in setting up attractive summer jobs for the players. Still others buy gifts and make loans and don't feel cheated if they aren't repaid. For their efforts they have a good seat at home games and the satisfaction of being associated with a first-class winning endeavor.

The number one member of the Athletic Committee is John Wilmer Galbreath, owner of the Pittsburgh Pirates, breeder of championship horses, and one of the wealthiest men in America. A close friend of Woody Hayes, Galbreath has contributed tremendously to the Buckeye success: "You want to know what my attachment is to Ohio State football? Well, you can't live in Columbus and not be a part of it. We don't have a big-league baseball, football, or basketball franchise, so the Buckeyes are *our* team."[3]

Here, as in numerous other universities, collegiate football has become a substitute for professional sports entertainment. The halcyon days are gone. The entertainment must be first-rate and that requires a sophisticated organization.

According to the National Federation of High School Athletic Associations there are over one thousand Ohio high schools currently playing football.[4] Each of these schools is assigned to one of the committeemen. A good player is spotted early and brought to the attention of the Ohio State brass. One of the most successful committeemen is Frank Lafferty, a motel man from Warren. Lafferty has been in the business of sending players to Ohio State since Woody Hayes began coaching there. In Lafferty's own words:

We don't lose very many that we really want. The idea is to keep after them and maybe help them find a summer job if they need it. Now, Paul Warfield, we got him a job with the state highway department. We got Van DeCree, our starting defensive end this year, a job with Public Steel. Randy Gradishar—visited him about 25 times before we got him—but he didn't need a job, his father runs a supermarket—do we offer any other inducements? Well, we're not supposed to do it, ah we don't do it.[5]

Another successful committeeman observed:

A good committeeman can find a way to help his players. We have a much cleaner operation than most places because we don't have to cheat to win. Woody has the name and reputation. Woody's name and the Ohio State Football tradition coupled with the *desire* of Ohio boys to play at

Ohio State University make recruiting a bit easier, even considering the ever stiffening competition from other universities.[6]

Like coaches at most other schools, the Ohio State coaching staff, under the direction of a recruiting coordinator, divides the state into territories. Designated recruiting regions in Pennsylvania and along the East Coast supplement the Ohio subdivisions. Coaches cover the areas that they know best—their home turf whenever possible. Since most universities utilize their coaching staffs in much the same manner as Ohio State does, the Buckeye recruiting success must be attributed to a winning tradition and the role of the athletic committee. Lew McCullough, who set up the recruiting organization for Woody Hayes, is now the athletic director at Iowa State. Like other successful recruiters he equates the activity with selling: "You have to know what the customer likes and dislikes, wants and doesn't want."[7]

Ohio State makes use of its former athletes in the recruiting effort. People like Paul Warfield, Hopalong Cassady, John Havlicek, Jerry Lucas, and Jack Nicklaus all do their part. Hayes himself used a strategy similar to that of Darrell Royal and other established coaches; he would calmly issue a challenge, something like—"Son, I know you are a hitter, but do you *really* think you have what it takes to be a Buckeye?"

ILLINOIS

I talked with Bob Blackman, then head coach at the University of Illinois, to see what it was like to recruit against the Ohio State machine. He cited the case of two boys who were very impressed with the University of Illinois program, liked the coaches, and believed the academic departments in which they were interested to be better at Illinois than at Ohio State. Blackman, elated, assumed that they would be coming to Illinois. But when he spoke to them, the boys replied something to the effect of: "We prefer you, your friendly attitudes, great environment, but we are going to Ohio State." Blackman asked the obvious question, "Well, if you like our program and the academic departments better, then why Ohio State?'' ''Well, uh, all the players we saw there had those Rose Bowl rings, and we just have to have one of those too.''

Blackman went on to say that he believed that *state pride* in Ohio, combined with the press buildup of the Ohio State image, has created some sort of subconscious desire among Ohio high school athletes to set their sights on Ohio State University. He contrasted the Ohio situation with that of the city of Chicago. There the typical high school athlete has little or no allegiance to the University of Illinois. Blackman correctly characterized the city as a crossroads for college recruiters from all over the United States.

The Illinois recruiting system is similar to those of other serious football schools located in close proximity to potential talent. Recruiting strategy is designed to obtain 80 to 85 percent of the required players from within the state. Each coach is assigned an Illinois territory and one out-of-state territory. Most of the out-of-state talent pools are on the fringes of Illinois—St. Louis, the Quad cities, southeastern Wisconsin, northwestern Indiana, and Ohio. The university also reaches out to New York and New Jersey. Blackman is of the opinion that boys from New York and New Jersey aren't as heavily pursued as those from Pennsylvania and Ohio. Most of them cannot meet the entrance requirements of the Ivy League schools, so the chief competition is from such schools as Penn State, Syracuse, and Pittsburgh. And there are more than enough to go around. Hence a surplus for those in the Big Ten who choose to recruit there.

Blackman discussed the differences between recruiting at Illinois and recruiting at Dartmouth, where he had had a very successful reign (104–37–3), winning seven Ivy League championships, and claiming one Lambert Trophy (figures 4 and 5). The Ivy League plays only nine games per season with no intersectional competition. There is no spring practice and there are no athletic scholarships per se, although a number of minority athletes can be ''recruited'' through the Ivy League's affirmative action program. Most Ivy League athletes attend school on a grant-in-aid. Approximately 35 percent of the total student body receive some type of financial assistance. Ivy League coaches do not engage in on-the-road recruiting, relying on the college alumni network for that function.

Blackman stated that in a typical year approximately one hundred potential football players would qualify for some type of financial assistance. Many who received it would not even turn out for the team once they arrived on campus. Because in a normal year over six thousand qualified boys might apply for eight-hundred Dartmouth openings, "the admissions people were always looking for something extra" — musical or dramatic ability, debating talent, or, as Blackman hoped for, unusual football skill.

Blackman liked the system but did not think it would work outside of the prestigious Ivy League because there just aren't that many outstanding *student*-athletes available. He went on to point out that even at Dartmouth, there was occasional cheating. In visiting the parents of some of his football players he discovered evidence of "C.P.A." — approved cheating on grant-in-aid applications. In one case, the family lived in a nicely furnished home with a two-car garage and the father ran his own business, yet the player somehow qualified for the full $4,000 grant-in-aid. Another boy, whose family lived in a small house, with the mother working and the entire family sacrificing to send the son to Dartmouth, qualified for only $1,000.

Bob Blackman was fired at the conclusion of the 1976 season. His Illini faltered after a fast start and once again finished in the midst of the conference also-rans. In six years Blackman compiled a 29–36–1 record. Excluding games with Michigan and Ohio State, he was 29–24–1!

He had no apologies: "Last winter eight Big Ten schools were working night and day to get average prospects while Ohio State and Michigan got the cream of the crop. The super blue-chip kids want a chance to go to a bowl and be All-Americans. When they visit the other Big Ten schools in the winter, they meet football players who haven't seen each other since November. But when they visit Ohio State and Michigan, the kids have just returned

Figure 4. Recruiting at Illinois (data base: 1974 roster).

Figure 5. Recruiting at Dartmouth (data base: 1971 roster).

from three weeks in a Miami hotel, yacht trips on Biscayne Bay, things like that.''

It was obvious that new recruiting strategies had to be developed by the other Big Ten schools. Their territories are being stripped of the best fruit. Ohio State and Michigan simply had too much tradition, money, and momentum in their favor. By 1980 Purdue and Michigan State were showing signs of improvement, but conference parity was still a long way off. The real move toward parity began when Iowa hired Hayden Fry, who immediately expanded the Hawkeye recruiting territory. Illinois brought in Mike Whyte, who established a strong California connection. Minnesota selected Lou Holtz from Arkansas, a proven winner with a national reputation. As a result the Big Ten has gained balance. New coaches and new recruiting territories have made a profound difference.

To truly comprehend the intricacies and frustrations of recruiting would require many hours at the side of head coaches and recruiting coordinators from a variety of universities. Realizing that such extensive first-hand observation would be out of the question, I thought a useful alternative would be to conduct an in-depth probe of one recruiting operation—that of my own university, Oklahoma State.

4
The
Cowboy
Quest

Ohio State is consistently near the top in college football, and the Oklahoma State Cowboys have spent the past fifty years trying to get there.[1] Oklahoma State, located in Stillwater, is a member of the powerful Big Eight Conference. Almost since its inception the Big Eight has been dominated by Oklahoma—since the mid-sixties by the Sooners and Nebraska. There have been occasional challenges from Missouri, Colorado, and Kansas and Oklahoma State, but Iowa State and Kansas State have staked an apparently permanent claim on the Big Eight football cellar.

Beginning with their 1969 performance, the Cowboys began a ponderous move upward. They finished 5–5 that year, but slipped back again in 1970 and 1971. The 1972 Cowboys went 6–5, turning in the first winning season since 1959. With further improvement the 1974 edition received a bid to the Fiesta Bowl, where they won over the Western Athletic Conference champs, Brigham Young University. In 1976 the Cowboys shared the Big Eight Conference title, defeated Oklahoma for the first time in ten years, and beat Brigham Young again, this time in the Tangerine Bowl. They had at last attained a measure of success, but it proved to be short-lived. The next year, 1977, produced a 4–7 season followed by NCAA probationary action for recruiting violations. The slide continued in 1978, a 3–8 season which proved that a long trek remains before parity with the conference powers can be attained.

The gridiron progress has not been without strain. Floyd Gass stepped down after just three years as coach to assume the athletic directorship. His replacement, Dave Smith, led the Cowboys during the winning season of 1972. Impressed by his success, SMU lured him to Dallas, leaving OSU in a temporary state of disarray. Jim Stanley, the defensive coordinator, was called upon to fill the void. Three head coaches in three years! Stanley was at the helm from 1973 through 1978. He was replaced by Jimmy Johnson shortly after OSU absorbed a 62–7 beating from Oklahoma in the season finale.

The great leap forward was accompanied by a drastic change in recruiting strategy (figures 6 and 7). Prior to 1969 almost all recruiting took place in Oklahoma and Texas, with occasional forays into Arkansas, Kansas, and New Mexico. Today, Oklahoma State operates a sophisticated and costly national recruiting program. The Cowboys still recruit heavily in Oklahoma and Texas, but the quest for talent in that area is incredibly cutthroat and mean. Oklahoma and Texas have traditionally had the inside track, so OSU has moved part of its search to other areas.

To provide an inside look at the process, Greg Mohns, former recruiting coordinator at Oklahoma State, agreed to maintain a log of his blue-chip pursuits. During the period of September 1974 through February 1975, he spent less than three weeks in Stillwater. His travels took him to small towns scattered over Oklahoma, Texas, Arkansas, and Kansas (table 2). He made two week-long trips to Chicago. He spent many days in Dallas and Fort Worth. Des Moines was favored by his presence on four occasions. In addition, he frequented Minneapolis, Kansas City, Little Rock, Peoria, and the Quad cities.

He assigned the OSU coaching staff to numerous filmathons the objective of which was to rate the potential of hundreds of high

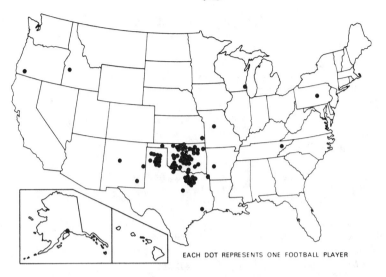

Figure 6. Recruiting at Oklahoma State — 1969 (data base: 1969 roster).

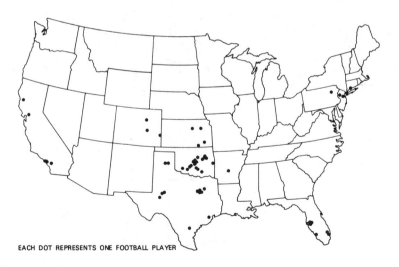

Figure 7. Recruiting at Oklahoma State — 1976.

Table 2: Mohns's Travels

Places	No. of Visits	Places	No. of Visits
Hooks, Tex. — Billy Sims	3	Peoria, Ill.	1
Tyler J.C.,	2	Minneapolis, Minn.	1
Tyler, Tex.		St. Paul, Minn.	1
Navarro J.C.,	2	Bloomington, Minn.	1
Corsicana, Tex.		Rochester, Minn.	1
Henderson County	2	Des Moines, Ia.	4
J.C., Athens, Tex.		Iowa Falls, Ia.	3
Dallas, Tex.	2	Marshalltown, Ia.	1
Lewisville, Tex.	1	Centerville, Ia.	5
Denison, Tex.	1	Sioux City, Ia.	1
Bonham, Tex.	1	Dubuque, Ia.	1
Plano, Tex.	1	Council Bluffs, Ia.	1
Grapevine, Tex.	1	Kilgore, Tex., J.C.	1
Arlington, Tex.	1	Caney, Kans.	1
Euless, Tex.	1	Pittsburg, Kans.	1
Grand Prairie, Tex.	1	Lawton, Okla. —	1
Ft. Worth, Tex.	1	Play-off game	
Irving, Tex.	1	Kansas City	8
Garden City, Kans.	1	Miege	
Hutchinson, Kans., J.C.	1	Lee's Summit	
Ft. Scott, Kans., J.C.	3	Rockhurst	
Independence, Kans.	6	S.M. North	
Coffeyville, Kans.	3	Hickman Mills	
Miami, Okla., N.E.O.J.C.	5	Moline, Ill.	2
Tulsa, Okla.	?	Rock Island, Ill.	3
Atkins, Ark.	1	Gary, Ind.	2
Little Rock, Ark.	1	Junction City, Kans.	1
Hot Springs, Ark.	1	Elk City, Kans.	3
Chicago, Ill.	5	Lexington, Ky.	1

Mohns spent 103 days on the road—outside of Stillwater—recruiting, not counting weekends during the season when he entertained instate and some out-of-state prospects on unofficial visits to the OSU campus, plus junior college official visits and weekends during December, January, and February.

school stalwarts. During the open-date week on the Cowboy football schedule, he dispatched the assistants to an even greater range of places, including New Jersey, Florida, Georgia, Colorado, and Arizona, so that they might assess the list of top prospects he had prepared.

Mohns himself put in many sixteen-hour days. When he wasn't seeing coaches, young athletes, or parents, he was visiting with sportswriters or helpful alumni. Countless nights were spent on the telephone in an attempt to open new doors and uncover that diamond-in-rough who had somehow eluded the attention of rival talent-seekers. His rivals also required some careful watching, especially during the time after a boy signed but before the lad's parents had okayed the contract.

Apparently no honor code applied prior to the time that national letters are signed and sealed. Anything goes when a prime prospect hangs in the balance. Mohns made two trips to Indian Hills, Iowa, Junior College to make sure all was going well with the three boys there who had agreed to enroll at Oklahoma State University. He found that recruiters from other Big Eight universities had been attempting to dissuade them, pointing out the numerous problems they would encounter. The boys seemed to be in a constant state of confusion, having heard so many conflicting stories. For the potential star athlete, there are just too many choices, and there is no way of knowing which one is best.

Recruiting is a frantic, hit-or-miss activity. It is difficult to decide where to go and whom to cajole. Hard work and frustration accompany the satisfaction that comes with the job. To illustrate the problem, I am devoting the rest of this chapter to Greg Mohns's 1974–75 recruiting saga. The September search was mainly confined to Texas and Arkansas. The first half of October was spent in Illinois and Iowa, with most of the activity confined to the Chicago area.

As described in the slightly edited words of recruiting coordinator Greg Mohns, the action opens in Hooks, Texas, hometown of 1978 Heisman Trophy winner, Billy Sims:

SEPTEMBER 2—Drove to Hooks, Texas, and spent the day watching Sims practice. Following the afternoon practice, Billy and I drove to his home in the country where he lives with his grandmother. We talked about football and OSU. I was fortunate enough to set up a visit date. Billy showed me 2 scrapbooks filled with articles covering his sophomore and junior years. Sims is a super prospect—a Terry Miller class. Drove to Tyler, Texas, and spent the afternoon.

[Terry Miller was the current OSU superstar running back who finished second to Earl Campbell in the 1977 Heisman chase. He gained over 1,000 yards his first NFL season with the Buffalo Bills. Mohns was certainly on the money in comparing Sims to Miller, and he appeared to be making excellent progress at this stage.]

SEPTEMBER 3—Went to Tyler JUCO and visited with Coach Andrews. He wouldn't let me visit personally with prospects and didn't want us to contact anyone until after the season, but he did invite me to watch film at anytime. Drove to Athens and Henderson County JUCO and spent the rest of the afternoon visiting with Coach Johnson and his staff. Watched practice. Leroy Montgomery, recruiting coordinator for Arkansas came by, and we talked while observing practice. After practice, I visited with the prospects which OSU is interested in and set up visit dates.

SEPTEMBER 4—Spent the day at Navarro. Talked with Coach Hern and staff, watching film and observing practice. After practice, I visited with the top prospects and set up visit dates with them.

[The Dallas-Fort Worth area is full of prospects and Mohns starts out as though he intends to sign the entire city.]

SEPTEMBER 5—Visited Hillcrest High School in Dallas and talked with Coach Garrison. He felt he had two, the best one being Rickey Rand, a TE & DE at 6'5'', 223, 4.8. I talked with Rickey and set up a visit date for February.

[The "4.8" refers to Rand's time for the forty-yard dash. This is a very important statistic for football players. It is comparable to a baseball player's speed from home to first and provides a measure of quickness as well as speed. A time of 4.4 is world-class sprinter speed and rare among college and professional running backs and wide receivers. Anything under 4.8 is very good for linemen and linebackers, indicating an ability to cover the wide stuff and play respectable pass defense.]

Visited Lake Highlands High School in Richardson, and met with Coach Bill Georges. He felt he had one top prospect in Mark Wilson, a Tackle at 6'4", 220, 5.0. I talked with Mark about OSU and we set up a visit date for February.

Visited Spruce High School and talked with Coach Bobby Lock. Kenny Pirozzo, our frosh QB, is from this school and Coach and I also talked about Kenny. Coach Lock felt he had one prospect in Tim McManus, a Tkl. at 6'4", 228, 5.0. I spoke with Tim about OSU and we set up a visit date for January.

Visited South Oak Cliff High School and talked with Coach Norman Hamm Jett. Coach said he had 5 prospects with the top prospect being Roderic Gerald, a QB & DB at 6'3", 180, 4.5. I talked with Roderic and set up a visit for February.

[Woody Hayes also liked Gerald and was able to lure him all the way from Dallas to Ohio State, where he starred as both a quarterback and a wide receiver.]

SEPTEMBER 6—Visited Highland Park High School in Dallas and talked with Coach Frank Bevers. Bruce Dewberry, a TE & Tkl. at 6'3", 198, 4.7 was his best player. I spoke with Bruce and set up a visit for January.

Visited Lincoln HS and talked with Coach Percy O'Neill. He recommended four players with Elton Garrett being at the top of the list. Elton is a TE at 6'4", 220, 4.8. I visited with Elton, and set up a visit for February.

Visited Richardson Berkner HS and talked with Coach Allen

Holladay about his top prospect, Doug Eidd, a Tkl. at 6'6'', 250, 5.5. I spoke with Doug and set up a visit for January.

I drove to Lewisville HS, home of Walt Garrison, former OSU great, and visited with Coach David Visentine concerning one of the top backs in America. Paul Rice is a 6'0'', 185, 4.7 prospect. He's a great one—I watched Paul practice and visited with the coaching staff after practice. Paul will not speak with any coaches until after the season. Coach has a bulletin board where he puts up all of the college recruiters' cards—as mine went up, I became #30! Harold Richardson of OSU was already up and so I was the second OSU coach to make the Rice board, although OU had 3 cards up. Paul is a super running back.

SEPTEMBER 9—Drove to Denison, Texas, and made it in time to watch the last 15 minutes of practice. I talked with Coach Goodman after practice. He had three. I talked with all three prospects and set up visits for February. Spent the night in Sherman.

SEPTEMBER 10—Drove to Bonham, Texas, and visited with Coach Jake Swann. Harold Perry, an End and Safety at 6'4'', 195, 4.5 was number one. Talked with Harold and set up a visit for January.

Drove to Grapevine, Texas, and visited with Coach Jim Cain, and he recommended two players, Joe Redman, a QB, and Mike Jurecka, a FB. I talked with both players and set up visits for December.

Visited Arlington HS and talked with Coach Bill Carter. He recommended three players, with top one being Billy Butler, a Tkl. & LB at 6'4'', 225, 4.9. I talked with Billy and set up a visit for January.

Visited Trinity High School in Euless, Texas, and talked with Coach Bill Bookout about his 3 top prospects. I talked with the three players and set up visits for them in February.

Visited Arlington Lamar and talked with Coach Eddie Peach. He recommended 3 players—Steve Bingham (LB & TE, 6'2'', 195, 4.9). Travis Milear (Center, 6'3½'', 220, 4.8), and Bob Perrault (RB, 5'6'', 160, 4.5). I talked with all three players and set up visits for Bob and Steve in January, and Travis for February. This was Travis's only free weekend as he already had visits set for Texas, Texas A & M, Rice, Texas Tech & Oklahoma.

SEPTEMBER 11—Visited Ft. Worth Poly and talked with Coach Clyde Tillman about his top prospect, Greg Hawthorne, a TE & LB who is 6'3'', 210, 4.6. Coach doesn't want any contact until after the season.

Visited Ft. Worth Arlington Heights HS and talked with Coach Merlin Priddy. He recommended 8 players. I watched practice and several of his recommendations appeared to be prospects. Coach doesn't want personal contact until after the season, but he did say that he would give the players my questionnaires for mail-back purposes.

SEPTEMBER 12—Visited Ft. Worth Haltom City HS and visited with Coach Joe Bob Tyler. He is a good friend of Coach Stanley's and we talked about his prospects as well as the OSU football program. I talked with all 3 of his prospects and set up visit dates for January.

Left Ft. Worth and drove into Stillwater to prepare for the recruits who were coming for the Wichita State game.

[In eleven days, Mohns had set visit dates for twenty-six potential OSU players. His next move was an analysis of the junior college scene in Kansas and Oklahoma.]

SEPTEMBER 17—Visited Garden City JUCO. Coach George Walstad is an OSU alum. Garden City has 2 prospects—Jerome Allen, a DT, 6'8'', 250, 5.0; and Clifton Payne, DT, 6'1'', 230, 4.8. Coach Walstad wouldn't let me talk to the players personally but said I could write them and set up visit dates through correspondence. He had a frosh, good-looking kid that Indiana University *had placed there,* but he wouldn't give me his name because Indiana University had placed him. An agreement, even though illegal, with another university apparently supersedes alumni loyalty.

Also visited Hutchinson JUCO—visited with Coach Matous and he let me talk with Denver Latimore—cousin of Moe Latimore, who played at Kansas State. Denver is 6'5", 240, 5.0, and Landris "Buddy" Cheeks, DB, is 6'3", 180, 4.7 or 4.6. I visited with both kids and set up a visit date for the November weekend that we play Iowa State.

SEPTEMBER 18—Visited Ft. Scott JUCO & talked with Head Coach Joe Hampton—who I discovered was a former Missouri University player—and we talked about a few people whom we each knew. Ft. Scott has a few prospects such as Joe Braxton, a FB who is 6'2", 195, 4.7—Coach has switched Joe to DB. Coach also recommended Leroy Harris, a FB who's 6'0", 214, 10/100; Joe Ristau, an OT who is 6'5", 240, 5.0; and Bob Weissbeck, a LB who is 6'0", 200, 4.8. Coach would not let me talk with the players but said it would be OK to set up visits through the mail.

Also visited Independence HS and watched Terry Davis, Dave Monroe, and Brian Turner. Monroe is a good-looking prospect—has good size & speed. His uncle lives in Stillwater and Dave wants to major in Agricultural Economics or Animal Husbandry.

Visited at Independence JUCO and met Jim Bohl—watched part of practice and talked with his prospects: Don Edwards, Clint Terrell, Tom Finnerty, Craig Lampson, Robert Sanders, and Herman Pruitt. I devoted some time talking with each player and spent the night with Coach Bohl and his wife—had dinner at the Elks' and talked football all night. He has 4 prospects that we are considering.

SEPTEMBER 19 — Drove Coach Bohl to work and visited with him some more — then I left and drove to Coffeyville, where I went to the JUCO and visited with Coach Cooper. Coach Cooper informed me that he didn't have anyone. The one prospect that I had on my list from spring recruiting had been suspended from the team. Coach Cooper and I talked about several of his freshmen who he feels will develop into players. Several were prospects that OSU had looked at in the state of Kansas but for some reason or another had not made the grade as a high school senior. After leaving the JUCO I stopped by the high school and visited with Coach Stockard, an OSU alum, and asked him about his prospects. He felt he had three. From Coffeyville to Miami, OK, and Northeastern Oklahoma JUCO. Northeastern had just been voted #1 National JUCO team in the nation that day. Coach Reuben Berry was very hospitable and visited with me about his prospects. He feels he has five good ones. Also a coach from Colorado State was there. UCLA, Colorado, and a few other schools were coming the next day. Watched practice along with Coach Berry in the rain and he verbally commented on each prospect. After practice I ate with the team and was introduced after dinner. Drove on in to Stillwater late that night. Friday I spent getting ready to scout Baylor at Missouri, while at the same time preparing for our game vs. Arkansas. Scouted Tulsa Memorial vs. Edison Friday evening before leaving Saturday morning for Missouri and Little Rock.

[Mohns manages to keep himself extremely busy, even during his infrequent stays in Oklahoma.]

SEPTEMBER 20 — After receiving a top prospect list from an alum in Arkansas, I surveyed the list and compared it to the information and names that we had. I assigned several coaches to scout ballgames in the Little Rock area Friday evening before the game with Arkansas. In talking with the coaches Sunday after the game, there were about five boys whom the coaches decided to follow up. So I decided to visit with them this week after our convincing win over the Hogs. I felt it would be good positive reinforcement to visit with them after scouting them and winning in Little Rock. Also there were some prospects that we didn't get a chance to see, so I decided that I would visit with them and try to evaluate their interest as well as talking to their coaches.

SEPTEMBER 24—Left for Arkansas. Visited Atkins, Arkansas, and watched a FB named Donnie Bobo. [Bobo became a star wide receiver at Arkansas.] We had seen him play Friday evening and felt that he was a top back. After practice, I introduced myself to Coach Leon Anderson and visited with him. I was able to visit with Donnie and talked with him about OSU. I had him fill out a questionnaire but coach wouldn't let me set up a visit date yet. Didn't want anything to interfere—I was the first coach that had been given permission to talk with Donnie and the coach didn't want me to "overdo it." After visiting with Donnie and Coach I drove to Little Rock for the evening and called and visited with some of my top prospects in Missouri and Kansas. Wished them luck in this week's game and told them that we were interested in them and we'd be following them this year (1st phone contact of yr.).

SEPTEMBER 25—Went to Little Rock Central and visited with Coach Young—he was busy and we set up a 1 P.M. meeting. Drove to North Little Rock, Old Main HS, and visited with Coach Henry Hawk. He gave me Freeman, Adams, Harper, Moore, & Skipper. Looks to me that Freeman, Moore & Skipper have potential. Coach Hawk had coached Phil Dokes, our outstanding defensive Lineman [now with the Buffalo Bills], when Phil had played there and we talked about the OSU season and Phil. Also met Phil's younger brother and said hello and visited with Danny Dokes for a few min. (No film was available to view because of exchange.) North Little Rock Northeast—visited with Coach Jim Crowson. We had scouted Andrew Love, a RB who appears to be a good prospect. Coach Crowson also mentioned David Nutt, a FB; Greg Lawrence, a DB; and Frank Wise. Nutt and Lawrence seem to have potential. Andrew Love's counselor pointed out that he is a step above Spec. Ed. and at present is only a 1.663 GPA. Has a chance to be a 2.0. It is a limiting factor, could be a detriment to him.

Little Rock Central—visited with Coach Joe Fred Young. One player that had looked good Friday evening was Jimmy Walker, a LB, 6'2'', 220, 4.8. [Arkansas All-American—1978]. Also visited about our season, etc., and he asked about Dokes and White and John Little, [NFL lineman from OSU].

Little Rock Parkview—#2 in state when I visited—talked with Coach Sam Goodwin. He recommended a Tkl., Jim Kissire, 6'3'', 220, 4.9; and Jerry Sullivan, G, 6'4'', 210, 4.9–5.0. He also felt that Charles Clay, a DE/TE was a prospect at 6'0'', 195, 4.7. I met Kissire, Sullivan, & Clay, and talked with them about OSU & let them know we would be looking at them. Also gave them a questionnaire to fill out and found out that Kissire's father is an OSU alum.

SEPTEMBER 26—Went to Hot Springs, Ark., and visited with Coach Bobby Hannon. We spent some time talking about OSU and the Arkansas game. This is James "Duck" White's high school. We talked about Duck and his success at OSU as well as his high school days. Coach Hannon and I discussed the ability of 5 of his senior players and two of his junior players. I tried to get Coach to tell me as much as he could about each prospect. The two junior prospects should be real blue-chippers. I left questionnaires for the boys with Coach Hannon and I proceeded to go to the counselor's office and visit with Mrs. Edith Irions, a counselor who is very close to Duck White. We had a fine visit and I left Hot Springs on my way to Hooks, Tex., to see Billy Sims.

[Mohns is becoming worried about his chances with Sims, and rightly so, since the Hooks speedster is being pursued by nearly every big-time school in America.]

I arrived in Hooks shortly before the team started the Thursday workout which was a light and short one (day before game). Coach

Julius Glossen from SMU was also there (black coach) and he and I talked about football, SMU, and OSU and Bum Phillips. Also talked about Billy and after practice both Julius and I spoke with Billy—one at a time—and I let Julius have the first crack. This was my second visit to see Billy and I just wanted him to know we are truly interested in him and I wanted to wish him luck in Friday's game. I made it a point to mention the visit date that we had set for January 31, February 1 and 2. He is anxious to visit but we need to keep him interested in us because he previously stated that he was only going to visit 4 or 5 schools, and at the present we are one of them, and I don't want him to cancel us and schedule someone else. Talked with Coach Coleman about Billy. He already had 685 yards rushing in just 3 games.

[Mohns brings in reinforcements.]

SEPTEMBER 27—Six of the coaches flew to Dallas to scout games in the Dallas–Ft. Worth area. I set up the scouting assignments in conjunction with Coach Richardson. I had a coach scout a game in which the top prospects in the area were playing. Most of all—we watched three boys I had visited with the past few weeks. We had six alumni pick us up at Love Field and they drove each coach to the ballgame I had assigned. First stop was Campici's Restaurant and the Egyptian room for some fine Italian food (beer, crabclaws, bread, and pizza). After the dinner with coaches and alumni, we went our separate ways to the ballgames. My alum was Charles Duty—a '71 grad in Hotel and Restaurant Management who is now employed as a recruiter and administrator for Brookhaven Country Club in Dallas. He was a great person and will be eager to help us in the Dallas area. He also was planning on going to Waco for the Baylor game. I scouted the Highland Park—Grand Prairie game at Highland Park. I was mainly interested in Bruce Dewberry of Highland Park. He had been a TE but moved to OT. He's green there but showed promise and has good size. I rejected both Danny Washington and John Tidwell of Grand Prairie. Neither one has the physical tools or ability to be a good major college player. After the game we all met at Love Field and flew on to Waco.

[Mohns decides to try Chicago. It's his first trip to the city and he goes in cold.]

OCTOBER 6—Sunday—flew to Chicago today for the purpose of screening the Chicago area for top prospects during OSU's open date. I sent the other coaches out on the road for 3–4 days. Their assignments were: Lance Van Zandt—cover top JUCO prospects in Kansas Lee Snider—screen Arizona JUCO's and area HS Don Boyce—cover top prospects in Colorado Hugh McCrabb—evaluate S.E. OK prospects Bobby Cole—evaluate top Florida prospects Harold Richardson—evaluate top Dallas prospects Gene Henderson— evaluate Florida and Atlanta prospects Jon Conlin—evaluate prospects in Northern OK—North of I-40 Don Riley—evaluate top New Jersey prospects Bill Turnbow—visit with top Texas JUCO's Doug Cathey—evaluate top prospects in Southern OK Wade Phillips—evaluate top prospects in Arlington and Ft. Worth, Texas Mark Hatley—evaluate top prospects in West Texas and Panhandle.

Don Riley flew to Chicago with me where he made a connecting flight to New Jersey. I got a rental car and drove to the hotel where I checked in and then drove to Thomas Sattler's, a Chicago native who received a doctorate in Education from OSU in 1973. Visited with Tom about top HS in Chicago area.

OCTOBER 7—I drove down to the University of Illinois at Chicago with Tom Sattler. He gave me a map of the city. I spent about an hour organizing my itinerary and plans for the week and also located all of the HS on the map. In talking with Tom, the Catholic League is known for its production of major college football players. So I felt it necessary to screen the Catholic League first.

My first stop was St. Laurence HS where I visited with assistant head coach Wally Sebuck who is also a counselor at the school. Coach Tom Kavanaugh is the Head FB coach but he teaches all day and it's Coach Sebuck's responsibility to visit with all college coaches. I spent about an hour talking with Coach Sebuck. There are 5 good prospects at St. Laurence this year. St. Laurence is ranked #1 in the state of Illinois and most coaches say that they are the best team in many years in Illinois. Coach Sebuck also talked about the other teams in the Catholic league and the top prospects at the other schools. I thanked Coach Sebuck and left my questionnaires.

My next stop was at Brother Rice HS where I visited with Coach Donnelly for a short time, as he was teaching a class. Coach Sebuck had recommended a LB at Brother Rice by the name of John Meyer—Coach Donnelly discussed John's ability and potential with me and asked that we didn't contact John until after the season. I left a questionnaire for him to give to John at the close of the season.

My next stop was at St. Rita where I visited with Coach Patrick Cronin. Coach happened to have a reel of film of their game vs. Loyola HS and I watched the film. I wasn't overly impressed with anyone but I feel the need for further evaluation. As we finished watching film, it was time for the players to report for practice and I personally met both Herman Kries and Manuel Williams and gave each a questionnaire.

I journeyed to Mendel Catholic HS and watched their practice. Coach McDonaugh came over and introduced himself and we visited about his top prospects. He recommended five. I believe two or three are bona fide prospects. His top prospect is a Tkl. named Mike Burt (who had just broken his ankle last week and is out for the season)—he was all-state as a junior and pre-season All-American at 6'4'', 230, 4.8. Mendel also had SE, LB, DE prospects. After practice I had a surprise as I was introduced to Tim Elliss, one of the assistants at Mendel, who I had played college ball with at Bradley University. Tim had been our back-up QB at Bradley and was commonly known as "Zeke." We had a nice talk and discussed old times and where everybody was. Tim has been at Mendel ever since graduation from Bradley. I asked coach if I could get some film, but all of this year's film was out on film exchange but I did get 2 reels of their junior year of play to evaluate. After visiting Mendel I decided to call it a day and head back to the motel, since it was 6 P.M. I ate a quick bite and promptly got on the phone to the *Chicago Tribune* office and asked to speak with someone who covered prep football in Chicago. I was fortunate enough to get in touch with Jerry Shnay who is in charge of covering prep football, and I talked with him about who and where were the top prospects in Chicago. He gave me some names to start with and said that if I would drop by he would type up a list and I could have it. So I made arrangements to meet him at the *Tribune* office the next day.

OCTOBER 8—I visited St. Leo HS and talked with Coacɪ Kelly. He recommended two prospects, a Safety and a NG. I left questionnaires for both of them.

My next trip took me to Mt. Carmel HS where I met Coach Jack Lord. He recommended two prospects, Bruce Hopkins who is 6'4", 235, and Doug Panfil at 6'5", 240. Coach didn't feel like Panfil had matured into a good player yet and was disappointed with him but was extremely excited about Bruce. I was able to visit personally with Bruce and we talked about fb and OSU for about an hour. He is very intelligent. His father is in the Marines (top brass) stationed in the Philippines. Bruce asked some great questions about OSU etc. and we had a tremendous visit.

Next I drove into the ghettos of Chicago and visited Phillips HS where I met with Coach Bonner about his top prospects. He has one of the best RB in state in Roy Parker, 6'0", 180, 9.5/100. Also recommended QB & DB Jo Jo Murray and LB Mike Clemons. I visited with the counselor before I left Phillips and found out that Jo Jo only had a 1.7 GPA. Roy and Mike's were over 2.0's.

I then drove downtown to the *Tribune* office and met Jerry Shnay. Visited briefly with him and took his list of top prospects. He also informed me that he was a graduate of MU Journalism school in

Columbia and that he hoped MU got all the *good* players (jokingly).

I then drove to Gordon Tech HS and visited with Coach Tom Winiecki at practice and he recommended four prospects. I left questionnaires for all of them.

Visited Lane Tech and talked with Coach Manasin about his top prospects and watched some of his practice. He recommended four prospects to me and I left questionnaires with him to give to the four prospects.

Visited Prosser HS and watched part of practice and talked with Coach Mel Lloyd about his prospects. He recommended two players but I rejected them on practice evaluation.

I was fortunate enough to catch both Prosser and Weber HS practicing in the same locale as both schools are only a few blocks apart and both teams practice in an athletic field located near a shared central stadium. I visited with Coach Jim Hoffman about his prospects—he recommended two players.

I got to the motel and started calling the coaches of the schools and prospects that Mr. Shnay had recommended and talked with several of them. Contacted a total of thirteen coaches and came away with a total of 25 prospect recommendations. To my surprise I spoke with Coach Ellwin Mohns of Downers Grove—he is related to my dad but we hadn't really known it—had a nice talk with him. The world is really small!

[Mohns spent the next three days running around suburban Chicago, contacting coaches and talking with and evaluating prospects. After a brief stop in Peoria, he then returned to Stillwater for a week to try and make some sense of all he had experienced since that first visit with Billy Sims on September 2.]

OCTOBER 21—I spent tonight calling HS coaches in Iowa asking them if they would please mail some film to me, c/o the Holiday Inn in Des Moines where we would be doing film evaluation of prospects on the Friday before the Nebraska game. The coaches who are going to help on this film evaluation trip are Hugh McCrabb, Bill Turnbow, Wade Phillips, Mark Hatley, and Harold Richardson. Charlie Alexander will fly one of the OSU planes up to Des Moines and I will meet the other 5 coaches and Charlie on Friday A.M. in Des Moines.

OCTOBER 22—Flew into Minneapolis, Minnesota, and visited with Coach Sheridan Jaeche of Marshall University HS and we talked about his three prospects, Mike Schellenberg, Matt Kangas, and Lyman Irwin. Coach feels that Schellenberg and Irwin are his 2 best prospects. I visited with both Schellenberg and Irwin and discussed OSU and its football program and *academic* programs. I also received 2 films for Friday's film evaluation trip.

[Apparently these were the first athletes who voiced a concern for the academic environment of Oklahoma State.]

From Marshall U. I drove to North HS and talked with Coach Ben McCoy about his top prospect, Rufus Johnson. I also received 2 reels of film. From North I drove to Southwest HS and visited with Coach Art Fredrickson and we discussed his two mammoth prospects Greg Murtha (6'6", 230) and Greg Cardelli (6'5", 245). I was able to visit with both Gregs about OSU, its *academic* and athletic programs, way of life, and Stillwater. We also talked about their team and its accomplishments (undefeated). From Southwest I drove to Bloomington, Minnesota, and visited Jefferson HS and Coach Patrick Waldner. He has four good prospects John Ruud, Tom Sapp, Tom Lovaas, and Steve Winum. Ruud is the brother of Tom Ruud, a LB at Nebraska. Minn. Gopher coaches rate John one of the best prospects in the state. He stated in an article that Tom's attending N.U. won't affect his decision. He is considering Minnesota, Nebraska, and Notre Dame. Made plans to pick film and OSU coaches up on Wednesday morning.

I drove south into Rochester tonight so I'd be up early to visit with Coach John Drews of John Marshall HS. He has an outstanding

RB and DB in Kent Kitzman who has rushed for 1,000 yds. in 8 games. I called Coach Drews and made arrangements to meet him before school at the dressing room.

I also called Kent and visited with him about OSU and hopefully we will be able to meet each other tomorrow morning.

[This trip was truly in the long-shot category given the fact that the Twin Cities are very short on potential major college talent. The Iowa junior colleges proved to be more fertile.]

OCTOBER 23—Got up and went to John Marshall and visited with Coach Drews before school. I then talked with Kent Kitzman and gave him a questionnaire to fill out. I then drove back to Minneapolis and went to Bloomington Thomas Jefferson High School and visited with Coach Waldner, had coffee with him and talked about his prospects. He gave me a film to take to Des Moines.

Flew into Des Moines—jumped in a car (Hertz) and drove to Iowa Falls, Ellsworth Junior College, where I met Coach Grover Garvin. Spent the afternoon talking with him and watching practice. He has several prospects but the top one is Dave Green, a Tackle at 6'5", 250, and a 5.0/40. I also evaluated Robert Scott, a Running Back; Scott Garner, a Tackle; John Blazek, a Kicker; and Dave Deal, a Defensive Back. I met the other coaches, Chuck Stanley (who was a Guard at OU in 1970), Jerry Albert, and Vern Thomsen. The High School and Junior College had a booster club dinner, and coach asked me to go as his guest and speak at the meeting. Before we left for the meeting, I visited with all the players and gave them OSU questionnaires.

OCTOBER 24—Drove to Marshalltown Junior College in Marshalltown, and talked with Coach Herb Taylor. He has two line prospects in Richard Lafford (6'6", 240, 5.0) and Lamar Johnson (6'4", 240, 4.9). Coach gave me a reel of film to take to Des Moines for tomorrow's film evaluation.

[You don't need to conduct tryouts when you can observe athletes in official practice sessions. Mohns learned much more in Centerville than he could have during many hours of film evaluation.]

I drove to Centerville, Iowa, and spent the afternoon at Indian Hills Community College. Visited with Coach Jim Spry. They are ranked #1 in the nation in Junior Colleges. The school that they were supposed to play this week canceled the game so Coach Spry had been having light workouts with a lot of running. Today he timed his players in the 40 and I stood next to him and watched the times. Coach Spry has six prospects that have a good chance to play major college ball. He has two big offensive guards in Matt Cumberworth (6'4'', 240, 4.8) and Ron Baker (6'4'', 220, 4.7), a Tight End named Percy McBride (6'2'', 220, 4.65), and Defensive Tackle named Curtis Kirkland (6'5'', 230, 4.7), a Defensive End named Wayne Mosby (6'4'', 205, 4.65), and probably the best prospect is Lorenzo Turner (6'4'', 210, 4.5, Defensive End). I visited with all the players after practice and then Coach Spry and I watched a reel of film vs. Oklahoma NEO in which they beat NEO, then ranked #1. I gave all the prospects questionnaires to fill out and mail to me.

[Baker and Turner both starred at Oklahoma State. The former now plays in the NFL.

Mohns spent countless hours viewing film, much of it useless, in the quest for OSU prospects.]

OCTOBER 25 — Picked up the other coaches at the airport this morning and we went to the Holiday Inn. There we watched film and evaluated all of the prospects that we had on film. I had received most of the film in the mail except the 10 reels I brought with me from Minnesota. We evaluated twenty players today.

After we evaluated each prospect and rated him we concluded our work in Des Moines. I mailed all the film back to the respective coaches and flew to Lincoln to meet the team for our game with Nebraska.

OCTOBER 29 — Arrived at Kilgore Texas Junior College and visited with Coach Charlie Simmons. When I entered his office he was watching film and I joined him to watch two reels of their game vs. Henderson County. After viewing the films we talked about his prospects. Victor Moore, a Line Backer at 6'4", 220, 4.8; Clifton Sullivan, a Corner Back at 6'2", 180, 4.7; and Dennis Tepera, a Defense Safety at 6'0", 178, 4.6. Coach does not want any personal contact with the players until after the season and said that he couldn't release any films during the season because of film exchange requirements with other conference schools. I left questionnaires for each of the players with him. Coach Simmons was very nice — he knows Lance and Wade [assistant coaches at OSU] and he hoped I understood the situation.

[Mohns frequently worked through coaches to get a line on the players. He also used them as intermediaries to arrange for further contact.]

Drove to Tyler Junior College and visited with Coach Billy Wayne Andrews. In discussion with Coach during practice he said he would help set up visits with the players. He said that he had arranged visits to Texas University on November 29 so I asked him about November 23 (our Iowa State game), knowing that Tyler finishes its season on November 16. Coach said it would be great and that he would talk with the players. Asked me to write them and invite them for the weekend and send the letters to him. "A step in the right direction" as we have been able to establish a rapport with Coach Andrews. Although I can't talk with the players yet we have set up a visit date.

OCTOBER 31 — Went to Hooks, Texas, again on my way back to Stillwater, and talked with Billy Sims at school today. Also visited with Coach Coleman. Billy and I just talked about their upcoming game vs. DeKalb and their chances to make it in the playoffs. Mainly I just wanted to stop and say hello and let him know that I was thinking of him and that OSU is interested in him. OSU Coach Bobby Cole had been to see Billy earlier in the week.

[Shortly after this visit OSU decided that they were out of the running for Billy Sims. According to Mohns, Sims's price was simply too high for the Cowboys to pay. Sim's dealings with recruiters had apparently made him well aware of his value on the major college circuit, and he was holding out for an offer commensurate with his rare abilities. OSU was either unwilling or unable to compete seriously for Sims's services.]

NOVEMBER 4—My Father's Funeral.

[Mohns spent the two weeks following his father's death rescouting the Kansas and Oklahoma junior colleges.]

NOVEMBER 27—Flew to Joplin, got in my car, and drove to Coffeyville, Kansas, Field Kindley Memorial High School and saw Coach Jim Stockard. Delivered some film back that I had borrowed to evaluate Kevin Pennington, who after evaluation I rejected. From Coffeyville, I drove to Independence, Kansas, High School and visited with Coach Mike Woolf about his top player, Dave Monroe. I visited with Dave. He seems real interested but Nebraska, Kansas State, and Arkansas are recruiting him hard. After having a good visit with Dave I drove to Ft. Scott Junior College and had lunch at the Pizza Hut which could have been called the Big 8 Meeting. Ted Heath and Bruce May from Kansas State were there as was Bob Foster, recruiting coordinator from Kansas University. This was only a couple of days after Vince Gibson had resigned and we talked about that. Ted and Bruce joked about helping them to find a job. After lunch I went to the Junior College with Defensive Coordinator Bob Shores and visited with Joe Ristau and Curtis Brown. Both had visited our campus last weekend and both seem interested in us. After talking with both players, I spent some time with head coach Joe Hauptman before going over to the High School and seeing Dick Hedges and Mr. Weatherbie [OSU quarterback Charley Weatherbie's father] who is principal at the Ft. Scott High School. They are playing in the state 3-A finals Saturday afternoon. From Ft. Scott I drove to NEO and picked up some film from Reub Berry to take back with me. From NEO I drove to the Sheridan Inn in Tulsa where Coaches Riley, McCrabb, Phillips, Richardson, and Hatley met me. There we evaluated film on the Junior College players from Indian Hills

Community College who were staying there in the hotel that night on their way to the Junior College bowl game [Wool Bowl]. We evaluated six reels of film and came away feeling that we wanted Lorenzo Turner, a Defensive End; Ron Baker, Offensive Guard; Matt Cumberworth, Offensive Guard; and Curtis Kirkland, Defensive Tackle. After looking at the film we visited with the coaches from Indian Hills and then I drove back to Stillwater.

DECEMBER 2—Flew to Des Moines, to go to Indian Hills to see the four players that we want. Tomorrow is signing date for the Big 8 mid-term transfers and I plan on staying here until I sign the Indian Hills players.

DECEMBER 3—Arrived at Indian Hills to be greeted by John Melton, coach from Nebraska, sitting in Coach Spry's office talking with some of the players. When Matt and Lorenzo saw me they got up and walked to the door and greeted me, a good sign! I spent the entire day with the players and talked individually with each of them. By 3:00 that afternoon, I had the signatures of Lorenzo Turner, Ron Baker, and Matt Cumberworth. Curtis Kirkland wanted to learn more about our Industrial Arts Department, so I called our Football secretary and had her contact Dr. Kiser. Asked him to write a letter to Curtis and send him some more literature about OSU's Industrial Arts Department. Curtis said that if he liked what he read he would sign with OSU next week.

DECEMBER 5—Went to St. Laurence High School—City Champ of Chicago—and visited with Coach Wally Sebuck. A coach from Wake Forest was there and we looked at film together. I made an appointment to come back at the end of the day so I could visit with the players. Jim Kozlowski, a defensive tackle and offensive guard, is great; Mike Ahern, quarterback; Bob Warner, a defensive end; and Dave Bavliska, offensive guard. I had tremendous visits with all four of them (individually) and afterwards Coach Sebuck said that had been the longest time that the players had spent with any coach — he said usually they got up after about 5 or 10 minutes and would excuse themselves. I feel I have a good chance at them. Everyone is after them.

[Mohns was overly optimistic this time. He lost all four and did very poorly in the Chicago area.]

Went to Mendel High School and visited with the great tackle, Mike Burt. We had a fine visit but after our talk Mike said that he has decided to stay close to home and felt like OSU was too far away, although he said he was interested in the school. [Few athletes made a clean break prior to signing day.]

DECEMBER 11 — After a week in Chicago I journeyed back to Indian Hills Junior College talking with the players I had signed. A lot of schools are trying to badmouth OSU and trying to get the players to change their minds. Earle Bruce (ISU) and Dick Towers from Duke were also there. Had good visits with all three players — Lorenzo, Matt, and Ron. All were a little confused but after spending the day with them I had things pretty well under control. They said things were great the day they signed but on Wednesday other coaches started badgering them and scolding them for signing — Missouri University and Ted Heath of KSU were the hardest.

DECEMBER 17 — Flew back to Indian Hills Junior College and visited with Coach Spry and Matt, Lorenzo, Ron and Curtis Kirkland. I visited with each player again to be sure things were going well. School is over tomorrow and all will be going home. Went to a basketball game and sat with Lorenzo and his wife and saw Indian Hills play at home. Spent the entire afternoon with the players.

DECEMBER 18 — Spent morning talking with the players again before they left for the close of the semester. Coach Charlie Cowdry of MU was there and we talked about football and the players at Indian Hills — he is trying to sign Percy McBride, a tight end, and

Wayne Mosby, a defensive end—both whom we have rejected, and I stayed there to be sure that he didn't talk with the players that I had signed.

Flew to Moline, Illinois, and drove to Rock Island, Illinois, and looked up Mrs. Turner—mother of Lorenzo—and visited with her about Lorenzo and OSU.

DECEMBER 19—Spent the day visiting with Mr. and Mrs. Jim Cumberworth, the parents of Matt, hoping that they would sign the letter of intent. Mr. Cumberworth was a Federal investigator—after four hours and a few phone calls to Coach Stanley, I had the consent of Mr. Cumberworth to sign the letter of intent but Matt was also going to visit Pittsburgh and Georgia Tech and his dad liked Duke University.

Flew to Chicago and drove over to Gary, Indiana. Plane was late and I finally got to Ron Baker's home about 10:15 P.M., talked with his parents and had their signature on the letter of intent by 11:15 P.M.

DECEMBER 20—Flew back to Moline and drove to Rock Island and visited with Mrs. Turner again. I found out that Lorenzo had gone to visit Ohio State and Wisconsin and would not get home Sunday or Monday. I became very nervous.

DECEMBER 23 to DECEMBER 30—Phoenix for the Fiesta Bowl—OSU vs. BYU. The top 300 prospects were mailed the following during the Fiesta Bowl:
Monday—The Fiesta Bowl Press Booklet.
Tuesday—The *Stillwater News-Press* Supplement covering the Fiesta Bowl.
Wednesday—A brochure on the Casa Blanca Hotel and on Phoenix.
Thursday—A letter by Mr. John Reid, Executive Director of the Fiesta Bowl, pertaining to why Oklahoma State was chosen for the Fiesta Bowl.

Friday—A copy of the game program.

DECEMBER 26—Called Lorenzo on Monday and after about 30 minutes he said that he was going to have his mother sign the letter of intent and that he was coming to O.S.U. but I will not rest easy until he is here. I made plans to fly up and see him after our staff meeting on January 2.

JANUARY 2—Had staff meeting at 10:00 A.M. and discussed recruiting and area assignments. Coach Stanley felt it was essential that I leave for Rock Island, Illinois, immediately to see Lorenzo Turner, and be sure that his mother signed the letter of intent, and make plans to have him move to Stillwater on Monday. So I left Stillwater and drove to Des Moines, Iowa, and arrived at 1:00 A.M.

JANUARY 3—After a few hours sleep I got up and left Des Moines, arriving in Rock Island at 10:20 going immediately to Lorenzo's mother's home. Lorenzo greeted me at the door and we sat down and started talking. I found out that Lorenzo had also signed with Nebraska [meaning that he had signed two Big 8 Conference letters of intent] but his mother hadn't signed, and that Coach Melton of Nebraska was scheduled to arrive at 11:00 A.M. I got nervous until Lorenzo handed me the Big 8 Letter of Intent from OSU with his mother's signature. She had signed it at 9:00 A.M. Relief!! We waited for Coach Melton to arrive and I was anxious to announce to him that I had Lorenzo signed. At 1:00 P.M. Lorenzo and I left because Nebraska had not arrived yet. We drove to the Holiday Inn and I checked in. We called Coach Stanley to inform him of the official signing. I spent the rest of the afternoon with Lorenzo and his mother. While we were at the Holiday Inn, Coach Melton came and was very upset when he learned the news from Lorenzo's mother.

JANUARY 6—Lorenzo and family arrived on campus and we looked at the available apartments in married student housing. They selected an apartment in the Brumley Apartments section. I helped Lorenzo and Toni move in and helped them to get settled. I took them around Stillwater and introduced them to many people. Let it be noted here that Lorenzo Turner is an All-American Junior College player and was MVP Defensive player in the Wool Bowl.

JANUARY 7—Flew to Chicago and drove to Gary, Indiana, to hopefully sign Curtis Kirkland and check with Ron Baker on his move to Stillwater. I arrived at Kirkland's house and was visiting when the mail arrived and he got his grades—regretfully his overall GPA was only 2.04 for 44 hours which made him ineligible, so Curtis decided to go back to Junior College and graduate. He needed 36 hours of 2.25 or 48 hours of 2.00 before he would be eligible. Went and saw Ron Baker and everything was fine for him to move to Stillwater tomorrow. He was flying in.

JANUARY 8—Ron arrived at Oklahoma State today—started enrollment procedures on both Lorenzo and Ron and helped Ron move into Iba Hall [the athletic dormitory]. Spent the day with them and oriented them to the campus.

[A rough day in Junction City.]

JANUARY 11—Called Donnie Edwards this morning and he said he wasn't coming to OSU; that he was going to Florida. I had Coach Cole talk with him while I went over to Coach Stanley's office and informed him. He got on the line and talked with Donnie. After the phone conversation, Coach Cole and I flew to Junction City, Kansas, to visit with Donnie. Donnie was at Ft. Riley playing basketball and we drove out and saw him and made plans to visit with him at 4:00 P.M. We went back to his house where we visited with his mother. She was upset and said she wanted him to go to OSU. Once Don arrived home, we found out that the school was Bethune-Cookman, a small black school in Daytona Beach, Florida. The coach had really sold him on Daytona Beach. We spent the next four hours talking with Donnie and finally agreed that Don would go and visit the school and then come back and make a decision on where to transfer. It was a cold day and when we arrived at the airport everything was closed. We jumped into the plane only to find out that the engines were frozen. We spent the next three hours freezing while Charlie, our pilot, and some mechanic tried to alleviate the problem. Wound up spending the night in Junction City.

JANUARY 12—Got the plane started and flew back to Stillwater without any heat—it was 2° and -20° wind chill.

[Mohns had to make sure that the Juco transfers were in the OSU fold.]

JANUARY 13—Walked Lorenzo and Ron to their first class to be sure that they attended their first class at OSU. This made their enrollment at OSU official—by attending first class they could not leave and transfer to another school (in essence, the same as signing national letter).

Drove to Elk City, Kansas, and visited with Dave Monroe and his parents. Had a great visit and Dave committed to me tonight and said he was coming to Oklahoma State. Drove to Joplin, Missouri, and arrived at 1:00 A.M.

JANUARY 15—Had breakfast in Kansas City with Dale Miller (he paid his own check). I then had an appointment to see Tony Corazzin in his home at 11:15 (Tony is a defensive end from Bishop Miege)—we had a good visit and then I drove to Rockhurst and visited with Mark Goodspeed during lunch. Flew to Chicago late afternoon and drove to Glen Ellyn, Illinois, and visited with Nick Mast, a defensive end from Blenbrook South and his parents. Had a good visit and Nick will visit on campus this weekend.

JANUARY 19—Heard from Donnie Edwards and Clint Terrell—Don had decided not to go to Florida or Southern Cal. and Clint decided not to go to Florida and both made arrangements to move to OSU.

JANUARY 20—Don Edwards arrived on campus. I flew to Kansas City in the afternoon and visited with Dale Miller and his parents for three hours. Had a super visit. It's between KU and OSU.

JANUARY 28—Up at 4 A.M.—showered, packed, and left for Student Union to pick up Mark Goodspeed so we can drive to Oklahoma City and fly back to Kansas City. Mark is a little slow and we're late leaving OSU and arrive a minute too late to board plane—it was just pulling away from gate. So we change tickets and fly to Tulsa by Frontier and catch another Braniff flight to Kansas City. We board the Frontier flight to Tulsa only to be greeted by Galen Hall of OU. (He's recruiting Mark for OU.) Mark and I sit in back of plane and when we arrive in Tulsa we talk with Galen. Arrive in Kansas City and I take Mark home and then I go to Hickman Mills to see David Fletcher. Next I go to Shawnee Mission North and see Dale Miller. That night I show two films to the Millers in their home . . . "This is State" and the 1974 Highlight Film of our season.

JANUARY 29—Go to Miege and talk with O'Gara and Tushaus and they tell me they have decided on four schools and OSU is not one of them (OU, Arkansas, Wyoming, and Arizona State). I am not real upset—didn't think they were really enthusiastic to begin with.

FEBRUARY 3—Went to Hickman Mills High School and saw David Fletcher for lunch. Lance Van Zandt and graduate assistant Mike McDaniel were already there from KU. Coach Frazier told me that David had told him Sunday P.M. that it was OSU but came to school today talking KU—"trouble"—I had lunch with David and he said that it was KU and OSU and by the time I walked him to class after lunch he was coming to Oklahoma State. I made arrangements to see him at 2:30—Meantime, I went to Dale Miller's house to visit his dad to see if any questions had arisen—talked with Mr. Miller and, at the time, there were no questions. I went back to Hickman Mills High School to see David—he was supposed to see me at track practice, but no David. He had left with Lance for an hour—about 3:30 David arrived with Lance and Mike—they had gone somewhere to see an alumni—David was totally confused by now, and Lance, Mike, and myself spent the next three hours watching him work out and talked with him. Then the blow struck—Jim Ragsdale, David's teammate who had signed with KU at semester (graduate in January), came to see him from KU and the KU bird-dogging began. David said that he would call Lance and myself at the hotel and let me know his decision. I went back to the hotel to wait for two calls—hopefully, Dale Miller's and David Fletcher's. David Fletcher hadn't called by 8:00 so I called, and his mother said she felt he was going to KU, but that he was on his way home. At 9:00 P.M. I got a phone call from Mr. Miller asking for me to come over! Great sign! I arrived at Dale's home to learn that Dale had decided to attend Oklahoma State. I was elated— then Dale went to work on David Fletcher—he called and talked with David for some time. David said he thought it would be KU. I made plans to be at Dale's at 8:00 for him to sign. Got a call at 12:15 A.M. from David Fletcher—he was confused and we talked. He left me with the option that if he called in the morning it was OSU and if he didn't it was KU. I've never seen anyone as fickle as Fletcher—he bounced back and forth today like a rubber ball. I feel he'll go to KU, although he said KU was out of his plans.

FEBRUARY 4—Big 8 Signing Date.

8:00 A.M.—I signed Dale Miller to a letter of intent. I was delighted—it had boiled down to KU and OSU and 7 of the 8 Big 8 schools had recruited him—only Colorado hadn't. The most interesting thing is that Dale grew up in Lawrence, Kansas, and had been a ball boy for KU for 4 years, up until the time he moved to Shawnee Mission this past summer. Everyone here (K.C.) was surprised—most everyone had expected that he would sign with KU. Dale is a Fullback at 6'2'', 210, 4.65, All-American, All-State and All-KC Metro and Conference.

11:00 A.M.—Called Dave Monroe at school and he had just signed his letter of intent. David is a tackle All-State who is 6'3", 230, 4.9, also All-Conference.

12:00 noon—Talked with Coach Frazier at Hickman Mills and Fletcher signed with KU that morning. His coach was really disappointed—He had hoped David would go to OSU.

2:30 P.M.—Picked up Dale Miller and took him home where he had phone interview with Bob Barry (WKY–TV, Oklahoma City), Ron Holt (*Stillwater News-Press*), and Tom Dirato (*Oklahoma Journal*) and Bruce Rice of KCMO–TV in Kansas City.

FEBRUARY 5—Went to Rockhurst High School and talked with Mark Goodspeed and Coach Al Davis before leaving for Stillwater. Mark visits OU this weekend and it's between OU, OSU, and Nebraska.

FEBRUARY 10—Flew to Kansas City from Oklahoma City and OU coaches, Galen Hall and Gene Hochevar, were on the plane. Got in to Kansas City, and went to Mark Goodspeed's home and talked with his parents, as Mark was gone at the time. They said that Mark was leaning toward OU. Mark came home and we talked. While I was there, Lon Farrell of Arkansas called 5 times, Coach Dick Foster of KU came by, as did Coach Hall and Hochevar of OU. I had dinner with Mark and his dad in the kitchen while Mrs. Goodspeed entertained the OU coaches. I feel that Mark is confused and undecided, and that OSU has a slim chance. I hope to have Frank Gansz come in from Pittsburgh and double team him.

[Coach Gansz arrives but Goodspeed checks out.]

FEBRUARY 11—Went by and saw Mark Goodspeed this afternoon. Talked with him before he went to track practice. He talked fairly good and told me to call tonight to set up Coach Gansz's visit on Wednesday. Picked up Frank Gansz at the airport and checked him into the hotel. I called Mark Goodspeed and he wasn't there but

Mrs. Goodspeed told me that he had narrowed his decision between OU and Nebraska.

FEBRUARY 17—Drove to Independence, Kansas, to see Dave Monroe and visit with his family. The main purpose of the trip was to take the national letter of intent to Dave and to make the arrangements for his signing on the 19th, or otherwise "close the deal." Everything went fine at Dave's and we arranged for the signing to take place around 2:00 P.M., on the 19th, at school. I would leave Kansas City as soon as I had signed Dale Miller and I would drive back to Independence to personally sign Dave to his national letter of intent. Spent the night in Independence.

FEBRUARY 18—Drove in snow to Kansas City and arrived early afternoon. I called Dale at home and arranged to see him at 7:00 P.M. Arrived at Dale's house at 7:00 and had a good visit with him and his family. He said he was ready to sign the national, but Brigham Young has really been applying the presure. (Dale is dating a girl he met in KC who attends BYU.) Dale's girlfriend has been calling everyday. So has her brother who is also at BYU and the coaching staff at BYU. Dale informed me that Coach Helm from BYU was coming at 9:00 P.M. to make his final approach. Dale tells me not to worry— well I am still at the house at 9:00 P.M. when Coach Helm arrives. I want him to know that I intend to sign Dale by my presence when he arrived. Coach Helm and I had met at the Fiesta Bowl. We talked the general coaching conversation for about 15 or 20 minutes when I announced that I felt it was time to leave. So I said my goodbye—and Dale told me to call him back in an hour to an hour and a half. I drove back to the motel and waited. When it was time to call Dale, the line was busy—it stayed busy and I became worried and jumped in the car and drove back to Dale's house. Coach Helm was still there at 11:00 P.M. I asked Dale to talk with me outside and I told him that OSU really wanted him and he told me he was 99% OSU, but he was still wondering at BYU—he told me not to worry and call him at 12:30 A.M. Drove back to motel—at 12:20 I called. Dale's father answered the phone and told me that Dale was really confused and that he did not want to talk with me or anyone else, and that he had decided not to sign until next Monday. Furthermore, he didn't want any coaches to talk to him until Monday and he would call the schools and let them know. Instant nightmare! I didn't sleep a wink— trying to figure out what had gone wrong and how to get him to change his mind. This is pure hell—worked so hard on Dale and now this—I had my game plan formulated.

FEBRUARY 19 – National Signing Date.

[Mohns utilizes Big 8 loyalty to seal Miller.]

7:00 A.M. —Called George Bernhardt, a former KU coach who is a personal friend of the Miller's and talked with him and explained the situation with Dale. I had met George on several occasions and he was also a close friend to Don Riley of our staff. I asked George if he would mind calling Dale and talking to him about the advantages of staying in the Big 8 Conference as opposed to playing in the WAC. Just as soon as I finished talking with George the phone rang and it was Dale. He told me that he was ready to sign and that he would explain when I arrived. What a relief! I dressed quickly and drove to Dale's house whereupon he signed the National Letter of Intent. Dale explained that he had just become nervous and he wanted to be sure he was doing the right thing and said he didn't sleep all night because he kept thinking about Oklahoma State and he knew that was the place for him. What a relief! (It was just like the groom before he was about to take the step into marriage.) I didn't even need the help of George Bernhardt but he did call, whereupon Dale told him that he had already signed.

Mohns's experiences speak for themselves. He won some and lost others. He faced many obstacles. He was harassed by coaches, girlfriends, and alumni. He wasted an incredible amount of time; his own as well as that of collegiate and high school coaches, the young recruits, educators, and alumni. He lost countless additional hours traveling, fighting battles that had already been lost, engaging in one wild-goose chase after another, and watching over a thousand reels of film. In total he convinced 134 youngsters to come to OSU for official visits. On balance, however, his efforts paid big dividends, as Turner, Baker, Sullivan, Monroe, Douglas, Miller, and Edwards helped immensely during the outstanding 1975 and 1976 seasons.

Mohns had a great many highs. Unfortunately, he was found guilty of a series of minor infractions; giving T-shirts and athletic shoes to prospects, and playing touch football with recruits, which, in NCAA terms, amounts to conducting a tryout. For these misdemeanors he was banned from involvement with the OSU football recruiting program for a period of two years. Furthermore, the NCAA decreed that the OSU football scholarship allotment be cut from 30 to 27 per year. After a year's stint as academic advisor for the athletic department, he was made an administrative assistant.

As it turned out, the problems associated with Mohns were just the beginning of OSU's troubles. The school was judged guilty of major football violations in 1978 and placed on a two-year probation by the NCAA. After the forced resignation of Athletic Director Gass in June of 1978, things got even worse. Jim Treat, a Tulsa businessman and disgruntled supporter of Gass, blew the whistle on what may be one of the biggest slush-fund operations yet uncovered in collegiate football.[2] Treat has alleged that many 1976 Cowboy footballers were paid between $50 and $300 per month. Funneled to the football brass by the North Central Oklahoma Business Development Association (the front for the slush fund), the cash was supposedly distributed to the players by members of the football staff. The jury is still out, but it appears that the catalyst for the 1976 success story may have been a seedy backroom bunch willing to put money in the pockets of "underpaid" athletes by any means possible.

OSU has fully recovered from the effects of its devious behavior. Under the leadership of athletic director Richard Young

(1978–83) the program was cleansed and revitalized. The 1983 Cowboys were 8–4, with a Bluebonnet Bowl victory. In 1984, first year coach, Pat Jones guided them to a 10–2 season, a Gator Bowl win over South Carolina, and a fifth place national ranking. 1985 saw the Cowboys at 8–4, including a Gator Bowl loss to Florida State.

5
Factors Affecting the Geography of Recruiting

For sports fans, poll watching is now a major national pastime. Just about everyone associated with college football and basketball engages in it. "We're Number One" is a ubiquitous chant often fortified by bumper-stickers proclaiming the profound message. The polls are accorded a healthy slice of media coverage and are argued and disputed with great zest.

The polls are by no means foolproof measures of excellence. Their accuracy is tainted by regional voting blocs—coaches and writers from the South voting for southern teams, from the West for western teams, etc.—and by the difficulties inherent in attempting to select the best teams on the basis of common opponents.

The whole business became particularly amusing in 1974, when the United Press International (a coaches' poll) chose to ignore the University of Oklahoma because the Sooners were on NCAA probation for falsifying high school transcripts. The Associated Press (a writer's poll), however, was not as concerned about the violation and ranked OU number one throughout most of the season, naming the team to the national championship on the final ballot. Confusion also abounded in 1966, the year of Notre Dame's controversial decision in its final game, against Michigan State, to sit on a tie in the waning minutes, playing out the clock with conservative running plays. Meanwhile, Alabama finished its season undefeated and went on to record an Orange Bowl win over Nebraska. When the final tallies were in, Notre Dame was selected national champion. Not a week had passed before bumper-stickers on cars throughout Alabama and the south were proclaiming the fans' response: "To Hell with AP and UPI; Alabama is Number 1''!

College football is vital to a great many people, but most schools and their followers will never experience the sweet smell of success. Since there are but two widely monitored polls, no more than two schools (and only one if the polls are in agreement) can be voted national champion. However, a finish among the top ten or twenty teams can also bring a certain measure of prestige and national recognition, and it would seem then that over a reasonable period of time most schools would have a chance to share in the glory. This has not been the case. Ever since the Ivy League de-emphasized the sport, thereby dropping out of the running for national recognition, college football has been dominated by a small group of universities.

The polls can be used to indicate the geographic dimensions of success. Darrell Crase, in a recent study entitled "Inner Circles of Football,'' found that only 59 of a possible 270 university football teams were selected to the top Ten between 1945 and 1971.[1] His compilations suggest that the rich, by regularly beating the perennial weaklings, are getting richer. Crase's study, based on AP and UPI polls, demonstrates that post–World War II collegiate football has been dominated by about 25 schools. Except for rare appearances in the top twenty, plus a startling upset now and then, the others have provided pretty meek opposition.

Bringing Crase's work up to date confirms the continuance of the postwar trends. Goudge developed a point scale utilizing both AP and UPI poll results for the period 1952–83.[2] From his findings it is evident that the same few teams have maintained a

Table 3: The Football Elite, 1952–83

	Total Points		Total Points
Oklahoma	733	Colorado	118
Alabama	731	Missouri	112
Ohio State	657	Illinois	110
Notre Dame	612	Florida	108
Texas	601	North Carolina	105
USC	583	Army	95
Nebraska	540	TCU	95
Michigan	504	Oregon State	93
Arkansas	439	BYU	88
Penn State	387	Baylor	86
UCLA	387	Stanford	85
Mississippi	341	Duke	82
Auburn	333	West Virginia	68
Michigan State	328	Kansas	66
LSU	319	Texas Tech	65
Georgia	303	Rice	63
Pittsburgh	300	Air Force	57
Tennessee	268	Miami, Ohio	53
Arizona State	208	Wyoming	51
Georgia Tech	196	North Carolina State	49
Iowa	189	Indiana	39
Purdue	183	Kentucky	37
Maryland	178	Mississippi State	32
Washington	178	Toledo	27
Houston	166	Utah State	26
Wisconsin	166	California	23
Miami, Florida	154	Tulane	20
Navy	152	Oklahoma State	19
Syracuse	140	Princeton	17
Clemson	137	San Diego	16
Texas A & M	128	Northwestern	14
Minnesota	124	Yale	14
Florida State	121	Arizona	11
SMU	120	Tulsa	11

Table 3: The Football Elite, 1952–83 (*continued*)

	Total Points		Total Points
Ohio	10	Eastern Michigan	0
Iowa State	9	Fresno State	0
Rutgers	9	Fullerton	0
Louisville	8	Hawaii	0
Temple	8	Kansas State	0
Memphis State	7	Kent State	0
New Mexico State	7	Long Beach	0
Utah	7	Nevada–Las Vegas	0
South Carolina	6	Northern Illinois	0
New Mexico	5	Pacific	0
Oregon	5	Southwestern Louisiana	0
Virginia Tech	5	San Jose	0
Washington State	5	UTEP	0
Dartmouth	5	Vanderbilt	0
Boston College	3	Western Michigan	0
Southern Mississippi	2	Wake Forest	0
East Carolina	1	Wichita State	0
Virginia	1	Brown	0
Ball State	0	Columbia	0
Bowling Green	0	Cornell	0
Central Michigan	0	Harvard	0
Cincinnati	0	Penn	0
Colorado State	0		

NOTE: 1,280 points would represent a #1 ranking in both polls for each of the 32 seasons. 64 points would represent a #20 ranking for each of the 32 seasons.

clear superiority (table 3). Eight institutions—Notre Dame, Oklahoma, Alabama, USC, Nebraska, Texas, Michigan, and Ohio State—have finished in the Top Ten more often than not. Another eleven schools have accumulated over 200 points. Many former powers—including Army, Navy, Minnesota, Wisonsin, Rice, TCU, and Syracuse—have slipped badly, failing to crack the Top

Table 4: Summary of National Rankings, 1966–85

Rank	Institution	Total Points
1.	Alabama	325
2.	Nebraska	295
3.	Oklahoma	283
4.	Michigan	273
5.	Ohio State	260
6.	Penn State	259
7.	Southern California	244
8.	Pittsburgh	212
9.	Texas	203
10.	Notre Dame	183
11.	Georgia	176
12.	UCLA	142
13.	Arkansas	141
14.	Houston	119
15.	Washington	105
16.	Arizona State	104
17.	Florida State	96
18.	Clemson	95
19.	BYU	88
20.	Auburn	83

Based on AP and UPI polls, 1966–85.

Ten since 1966. Their places have been taken by Houston, Colorado, Arizona State, Florida, and, most recently, Pittsburgh and BYU.

The last ten years present striking testimony to the concentration of power (table 4). Nine schools have amassed over 200 points, an average of a Top Ten finish for *each* season. On the other hand, forty-nine schools recorded at least on one Top Twenty finish during the period, confirming the balance that is slowly developing in major college football.

Once a university has built a reputation for football excellence, success tends to be self-perpetuating. It is not difficult to see why

Table 5: Television Appearances, 1952–83

	National	Regional		National	Regional
Notre Dame	42	26	Air Force	4	19
Texas	37	26	Boston College	4	13
USC	36	21	Colorado	4	16
Alabama	34	16	Florida State	4	18
UCLA	33	23	Texas Tech	4	21
Army	32	15	Wisconsin	4	22
Navy	32	16	North Carolina	3	29
Oklahoma	30	26	Oregon	3	17
Michigan	28	28	Arizona State	2	15
Ohio State	28	28	BYU	2	20
Nebraska	23	20	Baylor	2	17
Penn State	22	26	Oregon State	2	13
Pittsburgh	21	18	Rice	2	11
Arkansas	19	28	TCU	2	9
Texas A & M	18	21	Arizona	1	16
Michigan State	17	25	Clemson	1	17
Georgia Tech	15	14	Kansas State	1	7
Georgia	13	23	Kansas	1	15
Miami, Florida	13	15	Kentucky	1	10
Stanford	13	26	Mississippi State	1	7
Iowa	12	18	North Carolina State	1	18
Auburn	10	15	Oklahoma State	1	8
LSU	10	22	South Carolina	1	11
Missouri	10	26	San Diego	1	6
Florida	9	20	Tulsa	1	11
Minnesota	9	23	Utah	1	8
Purdue	9	28	Vanderbilt	1	5
Tennessee	8	19	Washington State	1	18
Washington State	8	30	Yale	1	19
California	7	24	Columbia	1	1
Illinois	7	29	Cornell	1	10
Duke	6	15	Dartmouth	1	15
Houston	6	12	Penn	1	5
Mississippi	6	17	Princeton	1	11
SMU	6	24	Ball State	0	0
Maryland	5	17	Bowling Green	0	4
Northwestern	5	16	Brown	0	10
Syracuse	5	19	Central Michigan	0	7

Table 5 (*continued*)

	National	Regional		National	Regional
Cincinnati	0	2	Ohio	0	5
Colorado State	0	8	Pacific	0	1
East Carolina	0	5	Rutgers	0	2
Eastern Michigan	0	0	Southwestern Louisiana	0	3
Fresno State	0	1	San Jose	0	11
Fullerton	0	0	Southern Mississippi	0	4
Harvard	0	23	Temple	0	1
Hawaii	0	3	Toledo	0	3
Indiana	0	14	Tulane	0	7
Iowa State	0	9	Utah State	0	7
Kent State	0	5	UTEP	0	0
Long Beach	0	0	Virginia Tech	0	10
Louisville	0	2	Virginia	0	4
Memphis State	0	2	Western Michigan	0	1
Miami, Ohio	0	4	Wake Forest	0	7
Nevada–Las Vegas	0	1	West Virginia	0	12
New Mexico State	0	3	Wichita State	0	3
New Mexico	0	12	Wyoming	0	15
Northern Illinois	0	0			

this is so. Success is synonymous with strong financial support, including donations for athletic scholarships, facilities, and training table supplies. Boosters with long-term loyalties result in sellout crowds. Television and the bowl game establishment also combine to benefit the elite schools. During the time covered by the NCAA television contract, excluding bowl games, Notre Dame, Oklahoma, Texas, USC, Alabama, and Nebraska averaged two national television appearances per year. Vanderbilt, Mississippi State, Wyoming, and Oklahoma State have not had that many since the NCAA began keeping television records (table 5). Television and bowl game receipts infuse large sums of money into the coffers of the elite, affording them an even greater advantage. Television revenues must be in part shared with low-exposure conference members, thus helping to keep them marginally competitive with the stronger institutions. In addition, the dominant football schools attract and retain the best coaches, or at least the best-known ones, giving them a real edge in recruiting. They have also developed sophisticated recruiting organizations and contacts, realizing that the perpetuation of outstanding teams is dependent on outstanding recruiting.

Primary Recruiting Ingredients

Recruiting of college athletes is both a social and a geographic process. From the latter perspective, the most elemental factor is the locational arrangement of athletic production, or, put another way, the location of the high school breeding grounds. Knowledge of where the potential athletes are is paramount to successful recruiting.[3] The location of the consuming points is also of vital significance to the migration of American athletes.

Recruiting involves a series of decisions of which the most crucial are made by the athletes and the coaches. The athletes must decide where to go; the coaches must decide where to search. Group decision making by university officials and governing boards, alumni and the general populace is also a part of the process. For example, a group supporting a particular school might decide to go big time and to enter the national recruiting scene; or, as happened several years ago at Marquette, the university community might decide to drop football and throw increased support to basketball. Such decisions, and others like them, alter the geography of recruiting.

The geographic pattern of athletic recruiting has changed markedly since 1950. Some of the changes have been forged by geographically remote universities like Wyoming, Utah, Arizona, Nebraska, and New Mexico. In their effort to go big time and to achieve national exposure through the medium of football, they have raided the establishment's recruiting grounds. Consequently, many new recruiters have been added, and, as a result, the recruiting game has become more geographically complex. There are now only a few schools— Ohio State, Texas, UCLA and USC— that can afford the luxury of the home turf search. And with greater financial resources at their command, they too are going national in an effort to stay ahead of the competition. Collegiate athletic recruiting is affected by many variables. Among the most important are:

1. The supply of athletic talent
2. The demand (market) for the talent
3. The social and geographical biases of recruiters and athletes
4. The location and attitudes of alumni
5. The athletic tradition associated with the universities in the marketplace
6. The athletic facilities
7. The reputation of coaches
8. The reputation of former players
9. Chance
10. University-associated Amenities.

THE SUPPLY

Athletic production varies considerably from place to place, with some areas growing many more athletes than others. This has to do with the way we, as a nation, have come to occupy and organize the space in which we live. Urbanization, suburban sprawl, and the rural exodus have had a profound effect on the geography of athletic supply. Supply differences also stem from regional variations in emphasis on football, basketball, and a host of other sports. Place-to-place differences in socioeconomic structure, and in ethnic and racial composition also affect the production of athletes. And, of course, there is the natural environment—most particularly, geographical differences in weather and climate.

To answer the primary ''where'' questions concerning the origins of athletes and to get a reading on their migratory behavior, a representative sample of college athletes was assembled. The rating system of the National Collegiate Athletic Association was the basic guide for selecting the schools to be surveyed. All of the colleges and universities to which the NCAA accords Division I, or Major, status were included. Several top-class NCAA Division II schools, as well as a few NAIA teams, were added on the merits of their performance during the last ten years. Most of the additions were made to the basketball sample, where the frequency of small college victories over university opponents is much higher than in football. Selection was governed by a team's long-term performance. One "upset" was not enough to warrant a small school's inclusion.

A total of 180 universities from forty-seven states and the District of Columbia comprise the football sample.[4] Each school included all of the products of twelve recruiting years, 1968–69 through 1980–81. The football sample consisted of nearly 35,000 players. The basketball statistics were taken from 240 teams with a total count of 9,500 players for the same twelve-year recruiting period. Data on each athlete's home-town high school, home county, metropolitan area if applicable, and race when available were painstakingly assembled from the rosters contained in university sports publicity booklets and in some instances from game programs. Information on each athlete was coded and punched for computer processing. From this information it was then possible to categorize athletic productivity for the United States and for individual cities, counties, metropolitan areas, and states.

Looking first at the states, we can see that a few states produce a very high percentage of the football players (figure 8). Texas, California, Pennsylvania, and Ohio are the leaders. Together they breed more than 40 percent of the talent, and each of them exceeds the national per capita norm. Illinois, New York, Massachusetts, and New Jersey are also important sources. The southern United States, Florida, Georgia, Mississippi, and Louisiana in particular, account for much of the rest. Most of the plains and mountain states are exceptionally low in the output of college football talent.

The data for college football player production at the city level show a high degree of urban concentration (figure 9). The Los Angeles and Chicago metropolitan areas together account for over 20 percent of all the players produced in the United States. Dallas,

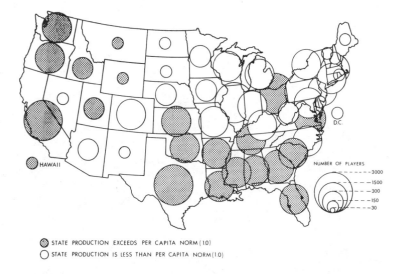

Figure 8. The supply of big-time collegiate football players by state, 1968–81 (data base: 1971–72, 1976–77, 1980–81 rosters).

Ft. Worth, and Houston represent a large percentage of the Texas boys. A region stretching from Detroit to Pittsburgh, encompassing Cleveland and a number of smaller cities, is also a gold mine for football talent. There is considerable talent in the eastern megalopolis, from Boston to Baltimore, but not as much as one would expect given the large population of that area.

Basketball is becoming more and more a city game. The metropolitan area of New York City alone provided over 7 percent of the country's "major" college basketball players (figure 10). Five other metropolitan areas conspicuous for the large number of players they send forth are Los Angeles, Chicago, Philadelphia, Pittsburgh, and Washington, D.C. The concentration of so many capable prospects in each of these metro regions makes them prime recruiting territories (figure 11).

A number of generalizations can be made from a comparison of basketball player origin on a state-to-state basis. Regional groupings of states with high and low player output are well defined

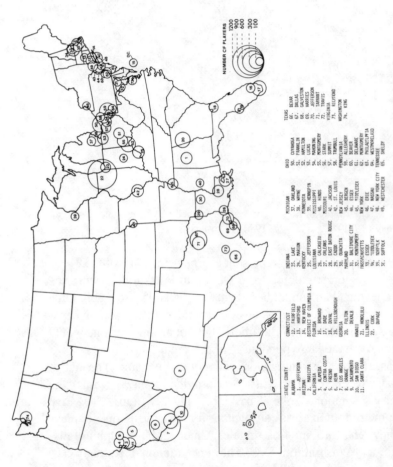

Figure 9. The major suppliers of big-time collegiate football players, 1968–81. City-county units which supplied 30 or more players (data base: 1971–72, 1976–77, 1980–81 rosters).

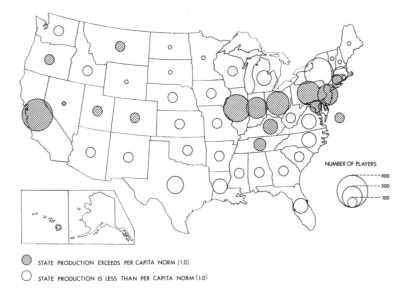

STATE PRODUCTION EXCEEDS PER CAPITA NORM (1.0)

STATE PRODUCTION IS LESS THAN PER CAPITA NORM (1.0)

Figure 10. The supply of big-time collegiate basketball players by state, 1968–81 (data base: 1971–72, 1976–77, 1980–81 rosters).

(figure 10). Our industrial states account for a great percentage of the athletes. The five most populous— California, New York, Pennsylvania, Illinois, and Ohio—are responsible for nearly 40 percent of the total. A corridor region stretching from New Jersey to Illinois, and including Kentucky, Virginia, and Washington, D.C. to the south, is the breeding ground for nearly 50 percent of the nation's major college hoopsters.

From a per capita standpoint Kentucky, Indiana, and Illinois are the source of a great number of players. Many of the athletes from these areas come from small communities where basketball is the major entertainment form and in some cases represents the focal point of the area's social life.

There are also noticeable deficit regions, places from which very few players come. They include the rural areas of the Deep South, the Middle Atlantic states, New England, the northern Midwest, and the southwestern United States.

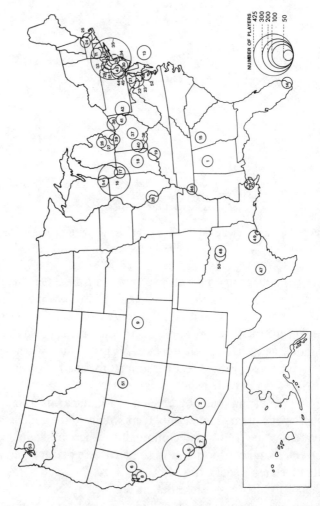

Figure 11. The major suppliers of big-time collegiate basketball players, 1968–81. City-county units which supplied 20 or more players (data base: 1971–72, 1976–77, 1980–81 rosters).

DEMAND

The second important recruiting consideration centers on the geographical arrangement of playing opportunities. These represent the marketplace. The market, which is divided into three tiers, has little resemblance to the general distribution of population (table 6). The so-called big-time schools constitute one tier, and they should be divided into at least two groups, the haves and the have-nots, perhaps based on the data generated by Crase. In addition to the big-time market, there is the scholarship-subsidized state and private college group. Finally, there is a group composed of state colleges and private institutions that do not provide athletic grants.

As with the production of football talent, there are substantial state-to-state discrepancies in the number and quality of collegiate playing opportunities (figure 12). Relative to the number of people who live there, the western states overemphasize big-time football. Arizona, with a population of slightly more than 2 million, contains two universities, Arizona and Arizona State, that have become top-flight national contenders in football as well as in basketball, baseball, and track. Most of the athletes needed to man the Arizona teams must be obtained from outside the state. Utah is an even more extreme case, with the University of Utah, Utah State, and Brigham Young all trying to field big-time athletic teams within a state containing only 1.7 million residents. In Wyoming (population 470,000), big-time sports have been developed almost wholly through the procurement of athletes from the Midwest and the Northeast. Idaho and Montana have also begun the move to big-time athletics by nationalizing their recruiting thrusts.

Overemphasis relative to local population also characterizes the New England states, the Carolinas, the Virginias, Mississippi, Tennessee, and most of the Great Plains. Underemphasis in regard to population is primarily confined to New York, Pennsylvania, New Jersey, and the Midwest, where the relatively populous states of Minnesota, Wisconsin, and Missouri each sponsor only one NCAA Division IA football team. In the midwestern states (excluding Ohio) where Big Ten Conference members are located,

Table 6: Per Capita Emphasis on Major College Football by States—1985

Rank	State	No. of Teams	Index of Emphasis*
1	Wyoming	1	4.31
2	Utah	3	3.97
3	New Mexico	2	2.75
4	Kansas	3	2.01
5	Mississippi	3	1.96
6	Indiana	4	1.85
7	Colorado	3	1.84
8	Hawaii	1	1.74
9	South Carolina	3	1.73
10	Oklahoma	3	1.70
11	Iowa	3	1.59
12	Arkansas	2	1.50
13	Arizona	2	1.45
14	Nevada	1	1.43
15	North Carolina	4	1.37
16	Oregon	2	1.36
17	Louisiana	3	1.20
18	Tennessee	3	1.16
19	Texas	9	1.13
20	Virginia	3	1.06
21	Ohio	7	.99
22	Nebraska	1	.99
23	Kentucky	2	.91
24	Washington	2	.88
25	Alabama	2	.85
26	West Virginia	1	.85
27	Michigan	5	.83
28	Maryland	2	.74
29	California	10	.73
30	Georgia	2	.63
31	Florida	3	.59
32	Illinois	4	.56
33	Massachusetts	2	.52

Table 6 (*continued*)

Rank	State	No. of Teams	Index of Emphasis*
34	Pennsylvania	4	.48
35	Minnesota	1	.39
36	Wisconsin	1	.33
37	Missouri	1	.32
38	New Jersey	1	.21
39	New York	2	.16
40	Alaska	0	—
40	Connecticut	0	—
40	Delaware	0	—
40	District of Columbia	0	—
40	Idaho	0	—
40	Maine	0	—
40	Montana	0	—
40	New Hampshire	0	—
40	North Dakota	0	—
40	Rhode Island	0	—
40	South Dakota	0	—
40	Vermont	0	—

* The index of emphasis for each state is derived by dividing the number of Division IA teams a state has by the number it should theoretically be supporting relative to its population. 1.00 = Norm.

there are only sixteen Division IA football teams, though the region has a population of more than thirty-seven million people. By contrast, the thirteen Division IA schools in the Rocky Mountain area are supported by just ten million people.

Many justifications are put forth by universities which have developed or are aspiring to big-time football, though two seem paramount. One rationale (perhaps it is subconscious) is to attract attention to *their* university and *their* place. How else could Nebraska, Wyoming, or Utah claim the attention of sports fans and the media in metropolitan America? The other reason is to provide entertainment in areas which lack sufficient population to support

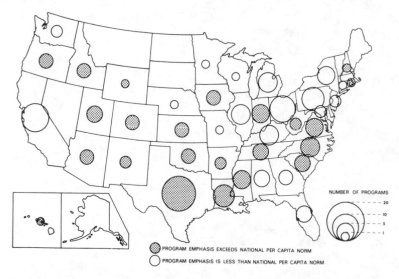

Figure 12. Number of big-time collegiate football programs by state (data derived from 1985 season).

professional sport or the theater. Collegiate athletics bring national attention to the area and provide high-quality entertainment as well.

The University of Nebraska is an example of what can happen. Lincoln, Nebraska, like several other places, now claims the title of "football capital of the world." Under Coach Bob Devaney, the Cornhuskers won back-to-back national titles. Devaney's ten-year record, at a school which had been out of the football limelight for nearly a quarter of a century, was 92–18–1. The university's football preeminence which has continued under Devaney's successor, Tom Osborne, has produced a change in the Nebraska life style. It has been a shot in the arm for the state in terms of prestige, the human ego, and even the economy. What is true of Nebraska applied to Oklahoma, LSU, Ohio State, Michigan, and several others.

Major college basketball also shows a great contrast between the player production areas and the areas that emphasize the sport

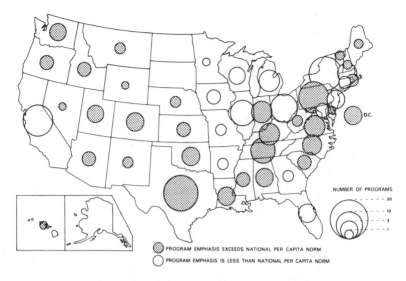

Figure 13. Number of big-time collegiate basketball programs by state (data derived from 1985 season).

(figure 13). Perusing the program map, one sees unusually high collegiate emphasis in the Carolinas, Virginia, New England, and throughout the western part of the country. On the basis of local population and ability to groom potential college players, several states greatly overemphasize college basketball, though to some extent this emphasis has occurred because of the chance location of private schools within their political boundaries. The region generally encompassing the universities of the Atlantic Coast Conference is illustrative, with schools like Maryland, Richmond, Virginia, Davidson, Duke, Wake Forest, Furman, and Clemson all competing, and most succeeding, in major college basketball. Even taking the role of the private institutions into account, however, the Atlantic Coast area shows an overemphasis relative to its current player-production capacity.

The other kind of overemphasis is epitomized in the Rocky Mountain zone, the approximate area of the Western Athletic Conference. As in the case of football, member schools of the WAC and other institutions in the vicinity are conducting athletic programs which can in no way be supported by the local population of high school talent. The region is providing more players than its meager population justifies, but there are too many programs for even such phenomenal per capita outputs as Utah's to fill the need. Utah has produced college players at a per capita pace of nearly two times the national norm, yet over half of the Utah collegians had to be imported from other states. Those in control of Utah athletic programs, almost certainly influenced by the Mormon concern for physical well-being, have elected to promote big-time basketball at all three state universities and at the one major private institution as well, a decision that has necessitated a vast recruiting program. Similar decisions have been taken in sparsely populated Arizona, New Mexico, Wyoming, and Colorado. The other mountain states, Idaho and Montana, are beginning to follow their lead, having greatly increased their competitive basketball ability during the last decade.

This emphasis is possible because of high player-production rates in other sectors of the country and also because a number of schools have chosen not to develop high-powered programs. The situation in the Rockies contrasts markedly with the relatively scant number of schools in Wisconsin, Minnesota, New Jersey, and even Illinois and Indiana which are attempting to compete in Division IA of the NCAA (figure 13).

The development of good teams affords isolated universities national recognition which they might otherwise be denied. It seems to make little difference to local fans where the players come from, as enthusiasm in the Western Athletic and Atlantic Coast Conferences indicates.

OTHER FACTORS

There is more to recruiting, however, than supply and demand. Many athletes do not move directly from high school to the college of their choice. A growing number are making an intermediate stop at a junior or community college. Many of these two-year schools now serve as "farm clubs" for major universities. "Gentlemen's agreements" between universities and junior colleges are commonplace. For example, a Division IA university will place, or stash, a young man at a junior college with the understanding that he will come to the university after his stay at the juco. The reason for this procedure may be grade problems, or concerns about the player's size or speed. A stay in a junior college is a maturing experience, an apprenticeship, that serves to prepare an athlete for the big time.

Recruiting at any university reflects the geographical experience and regional biases of its coaches. Where are the coaches from? Where did they play college ball? The strength of their contacts with other areas must also be assessed. For example, take the preference for Michigan boys by Wyoming or the recruitment of Angelenos to Utah—both may simply reflect the coach's geographical experience.

We must also consider the effects of an increasingly popular game; "musical chairs for coaches." The rosters of some of our major universities make evident the fact that coaching mobility has had a substantial effect on the geography of recruiting. Johnny Majors moves to Iowa State and suddenly there is a stampede of southern boys into Ames; when Majors switches to Pittsburgh the same thing happens there. Bob Devaney, in building the Wyoming program, imported scores of midwesterners; later, at Nebraska, he recruited the same area and added California to his territory as well. Frank Kush built the Arizona State juggernaut with Pennsylvania boys from his home region. The footloose behavior of coaches has undoubtedly been a major contributor to the development of nationally oriented recruiting.

On the other hand, recruiters frequently have rigid attitudes regarding the origins of the best athletes. These attitudes are related to their own place experiences and in many instances reflect their own place pride. A recruiter who is strongly attached to his state or culture region is unlikely to leave that region for recruitment purposes. Most Texas coaches are inclined toward the merits of Texas football players. Ohioans are partial to the boys from their state and to neighboring Pennsylvanians. Turning it over, an athlete who is strongly attached to his area will be reluctant to select a school outside it. Note that this was true in the case of Mildren, Cefalo, and many of the boys that Greg Mohns sought.

Alumni and friends of the university play a large (but difficult to measure), role in the recruiting game. They donate funds, aircraft, and whatever else is needed by *their* school to overcome the impediments created by distance. They provide summer and postgraduate jobs, sometimes cars and clothing, and numerous other favors. Their geographical distribution and reputation are also significant.

A dispersed group of alums can sometimes be more effective than a group situated almost exclusively within the ''home'' region. Notre Dame and armed forces academies alumni have ready access to all of the chief supply areas. The Notre Dame radio and television network is another powerful recruiting factor. It demonstrates alumni strength as well as the overall Catholic affection for the university, which has produced myriad subway alums in all sections of the United States. Notre Dame replays are aired in nearly half of all U.S. TV market areas. Reaching nearly every section of the country, the Notre Dame network has been a formidable influence, immersing unsuspecting athletes in the lore that constitutes the Fighting Irish football legend.[5]

Athletes are influenced by a multitude of forces. Where they go may be closely tied to the availability and quality of local collegiate playing opportunities. Do they have a strong affinity for their own area? Do they believe that their state institution is the ''greatest''? Do they have strong inclinations to live somewhere else? Perhaps they prefer a warmer climate, or a big city, or a place to hunt and fish. They must also deal with their own place pride.

A university's athletic tradition provides an edge in recruiting and must be reckoned with in any national assessment. Winners have definite advantages where the acquisition of young athletes is concerned. ''Son, we are offering you an opportunity to become a part of the Husker [or Sooner, or Fighting Irish, or Trojan] family.'' Contrasted to ''Son, we are giving you a chance to grow with a developing program,'' which is apt to be the more appealing offer? For most youngsters the winners just have a lot more going for them, and a place like Notre Dame is in a class by itself.

Tradition is frequently associated with a famous coach. When names like Barry, Woody, or Bo are mentioned, most people don't need any other identification. But how many young athletes know Earle Bruce, Pat Jones, Gaylen Hall, or Fisher Deberry, each of whom coached top-notch teams in 1984 and 1985? The celebrity value associated with a big-name coach cannot be ignored.

I have already alluded to coaching mobility. This propensity to flit from one school to another fosters subtle changes in the geographical dimensions of recruiting, as coaches tend to comb areas with which they are most familiar. Coaching switches of the late 1970s and early 1980s are generating significant changes in football recruiting. Majors has returned to Tennessee, Hatfield to Arkansas, Akers to Texas. Holtz has moved from Arkansas to Minnesota to Notre Dame. Jimmy Johnson made the switch from Oklahoma State to Miami as Schnellenberger departed for Louisville after an ill-fated USFL experience. Does that herald the northward movement of Texans and Floridians? Will Texas begin to intensify its search for foreigners and will Arkansas move its search west? The point is obvious. Coaches are so geographically unstable and have broadened their regional horizons to such an extent that the majority are now likely to think in terms of national recruiting.

Conference regulations also have a bearing on the national character of the recruiting game. Some allow more scholarships than others, and some promote redshirting while others do not. The poor showing of the Big Ten since the mid-sixties is in part attributable to a lower scholarship allowance (grants were restricted to thirty per year during the period that their competitors were awarding forty-five to fifty), and to a long-term ban on redshirting (legalized in 1973). They lost a great many prospects to the Big Eight and the Western Athletic Conference, both of which had more liberal rules. Academic standards also vary, and those schools with lower requirements have a much larger talent pool from which to choose.

Extra inducements, although illegal, provide an unfair advantage to those who give them. Typical inducements include automobiles, clothing, charge accounts, stereos, and hard cash. Issuing free game tickets to athletes for the purpose of resale is a common means of providing extra cash. The practice is especially lucrative at schools where games are regularly sold out and has been known to generate seasonal income in excess of $2,000 per athlete. Promises of postgraduate employment (summer jobs are legal) are also frequently thrown in. It is impossible to pinpoint the extent of the violations, but it is safe to conclude that they play a key role in recruiting at many institutions.

6
The National
Dimensions of
Football Recruiting

By collating the data on state production and consumption of football talent, we can divide the United States into surplus and deficit areas (figure 14).

Those states unable to generate their own supply of players must take the excess from those who produce more. At the extreme, New Jersey generated almost five times as many players as it could consume based on the number of big-time programs it sponsors, and Pennsylvania and Florida produced in excess of twice their own requirements. At the other extreme, Utah, Wyoming, and South Carolina together were able to supply less than 40 percent of their own need. From the pattern of surpluses and deficits portrayed on the map we would anticipate a great flow from the East and Midwest to the Atlantic Coast, the Plains, and the West. We might also expect California to export a substantial number of players.

The map pinpoints the cause of the great pilgrimage of youthful footballers to colleges scattered throughout the United States. In short, the supply areas are often far removed from the demand points for football players. Football players travel to provide their

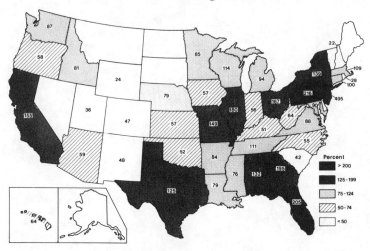

Figure 14. State surplus and deficits of big-time collegiate football talent (data base: 1971–72, 1976–77, 1980–81 rosters). Numbers indicate the percentage of its own needs supplied by each state.

Table 7: Leading Exporters of Football Talent, 1969–81

Rank	State	Total Production	Exports	Percent Exported
1	California	3661	1754	48
2	Ohio	2526	1472	58
3	Pennsylvania	2009	1367	68
4	New Jersey	1133	987	88
5	New York	1235	943	76
6	Texas	3514	926	27
7	Illinois	1543	914	59
8	Florida	1450	874	60
9	Georgia	986	730	74
10	Massachusetts	939	471	50

services wherever they are required. Their movement is not unlike the funneling of showgirls and dancers to Las Vegas and New York and aspiring actors to Broadway and Hollywood, or the shipment of steel from the Pittsburgh mines to the automobile factories in Detroit (table 7).

When we subdivide the United States into nine supply and demand sectors, it becomes apparent that this is exactly what is happening (figure 15). The most important export areas are Pennsylvania-Ohio, California, the Midwest, and the Northeast. The Pennsylvania-Ohio region is the chief donor to the South Atlantic universities, particularly members of the Atlantic Coast Conference, and a major exporter to the Northeast, the Midwest, and the West. Pennsylvania, which loses 68 percent of its high school players to universities in other states, is a leading source of athletes for the Atlantic Coast and Southern conferences, the Ivy League, Indiana, Florida, and even Arizona (figure 16). In fact, there were Pennsylvanians playing in all but two of the states with big-league recruiting budgets.

Ohio retains more of its best high school football players than does Pennsylvania (figure 17). The state provides a greater number of major college playing opportunities than Pennsylvania and relies heavily on its own schoolboy population. But despite the local opportunities, almost 1,500, or 58 percent, of the best prospects managed to sign with out-of-state schools, making Ohio the nation's second-ranking exporter of gridiron talent. Kentucky, Indiana, and Michigan are the leading consumers of the Ohio surplus, but Illinois, Virginia, West Virginia, and Kansas have also been formidable raiders. The Pennsylvania-Ohio trade is surprisingly low (74 Pennsylvanians to Ohio, 52 Ohioans to Pennsylvania), considering the intensive recruiting that characterizes the Ohio State, Pittsburgh, and Penn State programs.

Most of the high school players who leave California are recruited by Pacific Coast universities in Oregon and Washington or by members of the Western Athletic Conference (figure 18). Big-time football would have great difficulty surviving on the West Coast and throughout the mountain states without the injection of

Figure 15. Interregional migrant behavior of college-bound football players (major colleges) (data base: 1971–72, 1976–77, 1980–81 rosters).

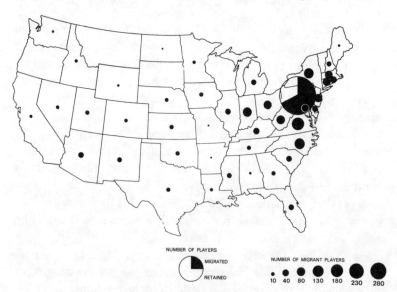

Figure 16. Migration of Pennsylvania high school football players to major colleges (data base: 1971–72, 1976–77, 1980–81 rosters).

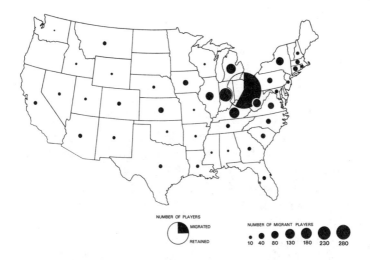

Figure 17. Migration of Ohio high school football players to major colleges (data base: 1971–72, 1976–77, 1980–81 rosters).

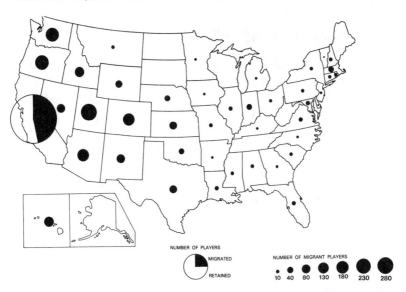

Figure 18. Migration of California high school football players to major colleges (data base: 1971–72, 1976–77, 1980–81 rosters).

California boys. It is noteworthy that California provides these export services while taking care of all but 11 percent of its own needs. Utah alone absorbed 169 California players, a full 16 percent of the exports. Oregon, Arizona, and Washington together draw off over one-third of the migrants. Colorado and New Mexico are also excellent California customers.

The impact of California decreases rapidly with distance. Very few recruits move east of the Great Plains, where Big Eight schools have shown a growing attraction to them. Notre Dame still gets a few, at least in part because of its omnipresent and persistent alumni. Even John McKay became concerned over the competition for his Angelenos. His location in the middle of Los Angeles, an abounding source of major college football talent, prompted him to call for a national reduction of athletic scholarships. I suspect that John Robinson would agree with McKay's apparent reasoning that fewer of the Angelenos would be plucked from the grasp of USC under those conditions.

The Midwest furnishes the bulk of the Big Ten's needs. It has also made a significant contribution to the development of the Big Eight as a premier football conference. Boys from the Midwest have helped Missouri, Nebraska, and Kansas to national honors and have done much to bring football respectability to the Western Athletic Conference. Even the Ivy League schools, particularly Dartmouth and Yale, have been aggressive in seeking scholar-athletes from the Midwest.

Illinois has provided most of the Midwest's regional surplus. Many Illinoisans, particularly the Chicago boys, migrate to Indiana, Michigan, Iowa, and Wisconsin (figure 19). The majority, over 59 percent, leave the state and this inability to retain the blue-chippers has often doomed the chances of the University of Illinois. Indiana has been by far the best customer, but Illinois's loss has also been Nebraska's, Colorado's, and Missouri's gain. Even North Carolina and New Mexico have profited from recruitment in the Illini territory.

Michigan and Indiana lose some of their limited supply of talent, primarily trading with each other, though a few boys are

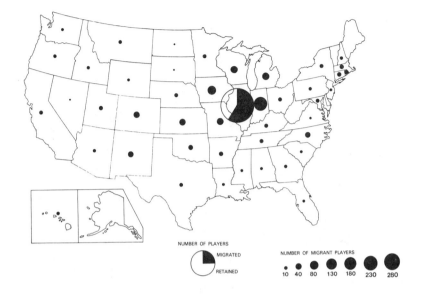

Figure 19. Migration of Illinois high school football players to major colleges (data base: 1971–72, 1976–77, 1980–81 rosters).

siphoned off by surrounding states. Illinois and Ohio actively recruit there, but without much luck. Three times as many football players depart Illinois and Ohio for points in Indiana and Michigan as those who make the reverse trip.

Those players pulled away from the Northeast usually matriculate at schools in the Atlantic Coast and Southern conferences or in Pennsylvania. The members of the two conferences are highly dependent on New Jersey, New York, and, of course, Pennsylvania talent. Over 88 percent of the New Jersey boys leave the state to compete, being widely sought after within the northeastern region. Their presence is also felt in the Carolinas and in the Midwest, particularly at Notre Dame (figure 20). Gridders from New York are also heavily recruited, with 943 leaving the state in the time period surveyed. As is the case with New Jersey, over 50 percent of them are drawn to the Northeast. Substantial numbers have been recruited westward to Ohio and Illinois and south to Virginia and the

Figure 20. Migration of New Jersey high school football players to major colleges (data base: 1971–72, 1976–77, 1980–81 rosters).

Carolinas. Massachusetts is a major supplier to the Yankee Conference and the Ivy League. The Commonwealth has had little impact in the Middle Atlantic region, but several Boston-area products have made the long trip to Wyoming and Colorado.

Only minor flows of players move out of the Deep South, Texas, and Florida. Given the number of playing opportunities in the Deep South, the region's talented players have shown little interest in other areas. Georgia, Alabama, and Mississippi are exemplary of the limited out-migration from the region. Georgia sent 195 players to South Carolina, 120 to Tennessee, 74 to Alabama, 53 to Florida, 57 to North Carolina, and 39 to Mississippi; the only nonregional consumer was Kansas, which lured 28 Georgians. Alabama and Mississippi were each other's major customers. It is obvious that most of the exports go no further afield than the culturally similar South Atlantic zone. Those Yankees who are invited down (Broadway Joe was one of the notable exceptions) seldom penetrate farther south than Tennessee.

Until recently, a substantial proportion of the southern exports were blacks moving along a modern-day "underground railroad" to schools in the Midwest. Big Ten record books document the accomplishments of many blacks who would have been denied the opportunity of playing first-class college football had they not moved away from the South. Today, though, the emergence of high-caliber football at predominantly black schools such as Grambling, Texas Southern, Alcorn A & M, Jackson State, and Florida A & M, along with opportunities to play at the previously segregated majors, has largely stemmed the tide of migration. Nevertheless, black players are still moving from the Deep South to other sections of the United States. Alabama blacks are going to Arizona and New Mexico, and those from Georgia are going to Kentucky, Kansas, and California. The most significant migration of blacks, however, originates in Florida and Texas. Over 30 percent of the Florida blacks have chosen to attend schools in Oklahoma, Iowa, Indiana, Ohio, Pennsylvania, and Texas. Nearly 35 percent of the Texas blacks are performing outside of the state, mainly in Oklahoma, Colorado, New Mexico, Kansas, and Arkansas.

Still, Texas employs almost all of its huge high school output at home. Those who leave seldom stray far (figure 21). Oklahoma alone recruits over 30 percent of the defectors, and much of the Sooner success story can be attributed to Texans, especially black Texans. The great Oklahoma backfields of recent years have been composed of Texas blacks, most notably, Greg Pruitt, Joe Washington, Horace Ivory, David Overstreet, Kenny King, and, of course, Billy Sims. Former Texas coach Darrell Royal became so incensed at the loss of such stars that he openly accused Barry Switzer and the University of Oklahoma of illegal activities in his territory. Since then, half the membership of the Southwest Conference and Oklahoma State University have been caught cheating in Texas. Louisiana takes another quarter of those who leave

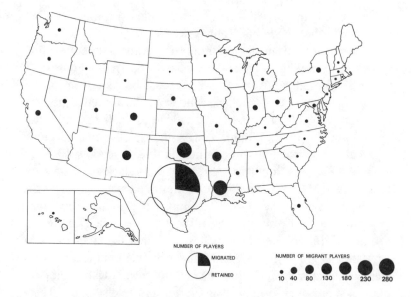

Figure 21. Migration of Texas high school football to major colleges (data base: 1971–72, 1976–77, 1980–81 rosters).

Texas, with most of the remainder dispersed among New Mexico, Colorado, and Arkansas. In contrast to Pennsylvania, Texas retains nearly 80 percent of its athletes.

Considering that the quality of Texas football has been well known since the 1950s, it is surprising that so few Texans leave the state. Apparently state loyalty is a very strong force in the lives of the young athletes, particularly the whites. With the spread of the Texas high school football legend, however, more of the best prospects are opting to leave, and the trend is virtually certain to continue.

Florida reverses the pattern of its southern brethren. Schoolboy gridders from Florida are competing in thirty-six states. Outside the South, they are very important to the football fortunes of schools in Texas, Oklahoma, and Kansas. Florida-bred gridders are also making major contributions in Pennsylvania, Indiana, New York, and Virginia.

More than half of the interregional movement of players is accounted for by the lust for football prominence among universities in the vast Plains—Rockies—Northwest region and in the smaller South Atlantic zone. Both areas are characterized by schools which are trying to field national-class teams as well as by a limited local supply of top-flight players. Consequently, more than 3,000 players had to be recruited into the western area and nearly 1,500 by the South Atlantic schools. Aside from the two large deficit areas, most of the interregional flow balances out, with midwestern and northeastern exports roughly equaling their imports. Nevertheless, the sheer magnitude of player migrations is indicative of the heated competition for, and the high cost of acquiring, football players in the present market.

The Small Schools

Though most of the attention is focused on recruiting by the major football schools, there are over 500 ''small'' schools trying to pick up the leftovers. Since a great number of professional players come out of obscure (where football is concerned) places like Jackson State, Grambling, Catawba, Augustana, Northern Iowa, or Langston, it is obvious that some of the best players are overlooked or cast aside by the big-time schools. But though much is made of each rags-to-riches jump from Nowhere Tech to the pros, most of the small college recruits are a little bit smaller or slower than those at the big colleges.

For comparative purposes I developed a 50 percent sample, one-half of the small colleges located in each state, involving a total of over 9,000 players. The geographical movement of players from hometown to small college suggests that recruiting on that level runs the gamut from very intense to what could be accurately termed nonrecruiting. The latter extreme is common at institutions that really play the game for the sheer fun of it.

Twenty-nine percent of the small college football players traveled out of their home state to compete (figure 22). Many of

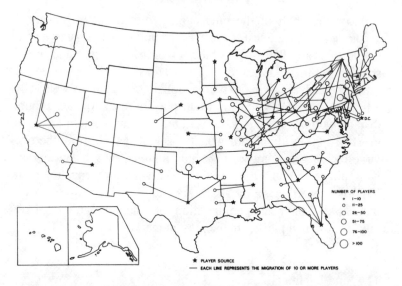

Figure 22. Actual migratory behavior of college-bound football players (minor colleges, as designated by the NCAA and NAIA and including a 50 percent sample from each state) (data base: 1971–72 rosters).

those chose to attend private liberal arts colleges, and in most instances the state affiliation of the school was of little consequence.

The big-name universities are much better than the small schools at overcoming the obstacles created by distance. Adequately financed, they possess the ability to recruit from all the lucrative supply regions, whereas the small state and private colleges are usually confined to their immediate locales. For example, Notre Dame has the financial resources to send recruiters to all the talent grounds in search of the best football players, but Slippery Rock must be content with the Pennsylvania products that Penn State and Pittsburgh pass by.

Recruiting Patterns of Selected Schools

As we have seen, recruiting at any institution is dependent on a

Figure 23. Recruiting at Ohio State (data base: 1985 roster). Each dot represents one football player.

multiplicity of factors—a school's location relative to the supply of talent; the whereabouts of its competition; the ideas of the present coach, as well as his prior geographical experiences and prejudices. Tradition and alumni support are also important.

The best way to appreciate these interactive recruiting forces is to map the origins of players from several institutions which utilize different recruiting strategies. In some cases we must view recruiting over time to really appreciate how the system functions. The geographical patterns that emerge from a study of selected universities illustrate the workings of the recruiting game at different places, for different coaches, and at different times.

The first set of maps (figures 23, 24, and 25) depicts the best of all situations, at least from the recruiter's standpoint. The pattern here can be appropriately titled "Going with the Locals," for recruiting at Ohio State, Texas, and USC is almost exclusively a local operation. Each of these institutions is situated in the midst of a football talent pool, and each has a great tradition, along with an outstanding reputation among the athletes it seeks. Combine this with a cadre of dedicated and well-organized alumni and friends

Figure 24. Recruiting at Texas (data base: 1985 roster). Each dot represents one football player.

Figure 25. Recruiting at USC (data base: 1985 roster). Each dot represents one football player.

Figure 26. Recruiting at Nebraska (data base: 1985 roster). Each dot represents one football player.

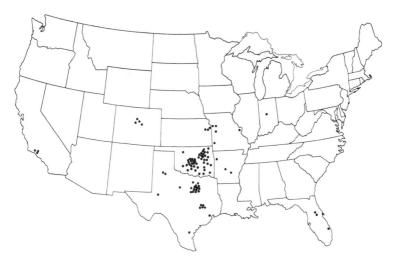

Figure 27. Recruiting at Oklahoma (data base: 1985 roster). Each dot represents one football player.

Figure 28. Recruiting at Alabama (data base: 1985 roster). Each dot represents one football player.

Figure 29. Recruiting at Wyoming (data base: 1985 roster). Each dot represents one football player.

Figure 30. Recruiting at Notre Dame (data base: 1985 roster). Each dot represents one football player.

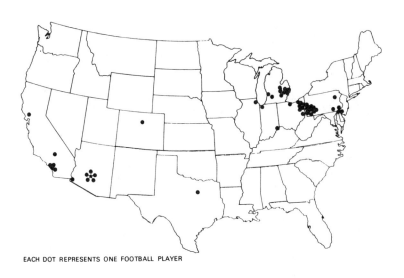

EACH DOT REPRESENTS ONE FOOTBALL PLAYER

Figure 31. Recruiting at Arizona State — 1962 (data base: 1962 roster).

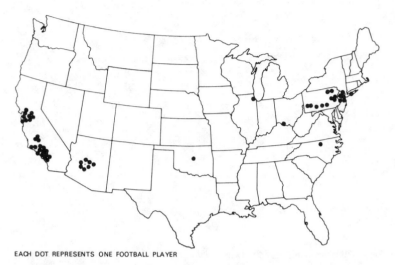

EACH DOT REPRESENTS ONE FOOTBALL PLAYER

Figure 32. Recruiting at Arizona State— 1970 (data base: 1970 roster).

Figure 33. Recruiting at Arizona State— 1985 (data base: 1985 roster). Each dot represents one football player.

and you have success—success in the recruiting game and in the national standings!

Nebraska, Oklahoma, and Alabama (figures 26, 27, and 28) epitomize a home-and-away recruiting strategy. Each combs the home area, generally beating the local competition (Nebraska doesn't have any) in the quest for the services of home-grown talent. Few of the prime state products escape the grasp of these juggernauts.

In addition to recruiting at home, Oklahoma raids Texas, Alabama harvests the Southeast, and Nebraska hits prime targets throughout the country. Since Joe Namath, Alabama has relaxed its ban on Yankees, but since it now admits blacks, there is little need for much recruiting outside the Southeast. Under Switzer, Oklahoma has moved far afield, to California, Florida, and points north. Nebraska has deployed its recruiting forces to Los Angeles, Chicago, Pittsburgh, Detroit, and wherever else a potential Cornhusker might be lurking. The system has worked well for all three.

Wyoming and Notre Dame (figures 29 and 30) are the best examples of what appears to be a scattergun approach or random recruiting philosophy. Wyoming does it out of desperation, since the state does not contain enough talented schoolboy gridders to support an NAIA team. Wyoming imports players from every place except the Deep South—probably because a southern boy couldn't survive an icy Laramie winter.

Notre Dame fishes the best waters with supreme confidence. As the national Catholic football institution, its tradition and reputation are unparalleled. Consequently, it obtains most of the people it seeks, whether they hail from nearby Chicago or Cincinnati, or from more distant football hotbeds like Pittsburgh, Philadelphia, and Los Angeles. The Irish also succeed in Texas, Oklahoma, and anywhere else their persistent alumni or followers call home.

The bulk of the blue-chip players, as defined by the high school All American selections, attend the top-ranked football schools. Sutton documented this pattern of acquisition in his study of blue-chip recruiting (table 8).[1] The best are getting the best!

The geography of recruiting at any institution can change sub-

Table 8: Blue-Chip Signings

Rank*	Institution	No. of High School All Americans
1	Alabama	26
2	Oklahoma	41
3	Michigan	33
4	Nebraska	22
5	USC	50
6	Ohio State	54
7	Penn State	39
8	Notre Dame	76
9	Texas	34
10	Pitt	17
11	Arkansas	16
12	Houston	14
13	Georgia	28
14	UCLA	36
15	Arizona State	13
16	Florida State	16
17	North Carolina	19
18	Clemson	10
19	Maryland	11
20	Auburn	14

Source: Figure "Signings of High School 'All-American' Football Players by 'Composite Top Twenty Schools,' 1972–1981," in William Sutton, "An Analysis of Blue Chip Recruiting," Eh.D. diss., Oklahoma State University, 1982.
Note: The total number of signees equals 559, or 56 percent of all recruits.
* Rank is based on a combination of both AP and UPI final poll results for the period 1972–81.

stantially over the years (figures 31, 32, and 33). Arizona State recruiting has undergone a major geographical transformation since 1962. Frank Kush built his early teams with the sons of mill hands and miners from Pennsylvania and Ohio. By 1970 he was getting most of his talent in California, though still relying also on the eastern front. Today the home boys are coming to the fore. Arizona high school talent has finally developed to the point that the Sun Devils can now recruit "home and away," like Nebraska, Alabama, and Oklahoma.

It is easy to see that everyone plays the recruiting game a bit differently and that a given school's strategy is dependent on its location, the location or existence of serious competition, and on the nature of the institution itself, as well as on the fickle whims of the coach and his supporters.

We have seen how some of the winners operate. Let's now move to regional combinations of recruiting behavior and examine the activities of selected athletic conferences.

7
The
Conferences

The athletic conferences collectively exemplify the recruiting behavior of their membership. Designed for the purpose of promoting athletic and other forms of competition (and sometimes even cooperation), the conferences are usually organized along regional lines. The Big Ten represents the Midwest; the Big Eight, the Great Plains; and the Pacific Ten, Southeastern, and the Southwest are named for their respective regions. Even in the major conferences there are often two or more members from the same state: Michigan and Michigan State; Auburn and Alabama; UCLA, Cal, Stanford, and USC; and the Texas schools situation are representative. As a result, member schools of the same conference are frequently in competition for the services of the same athletes.

Generally speaking, the successful conferences (the Big Eight is an exception) are those located in the midst of talent pools. For the period 1945–1978, the Big Ten and Southeastern conferences have dominated the national rankings (table 9). There has been much more balance within these two, as well as in the Pacific Ten, Big Eight, and Southwest, since 1970. And although the Atlantic Coast, Western Athletic, Missouri Valley, and Big Sky have

The Conferences

Table 9: Conference Prestige[1]

	1945–78	Balance Rating[2]	1973–83	Balance Rating
Southeast	82	63	43	54
Big Ten	78	35	28	29
Southwest	54	43	27	32
Big Eight	52	31	29	26
Pacific Ten	49	39	32	33
Atlantic Coast	23	57	18	55
Western Athletic	10	30	10	30
Mid America	4	25	4	13

[1]Based on number of finishes in the Top 10, 1945–71, and the Top 20, 1973–83. One point is awarded to each conference member for each Top 10 finish, between 1945 and 1971, and each Top 20 finish thereafter.

[2]The higher the rating the greater the balance between the conference's best and worst teams. For example, the low ratings, 31 and 26, for the Big Eight are indicative of the conference dominance by Oklahoma and Nebraska. At the other extreme the Southeastern Conference ratings of 63 and 54 point out the fact that the majority of its members have ranked high nationally.

national recruiting programs, they have not yet been able to muster the organization necessary to overcome the deficiencies of their talent-shy locations. An Ohio State type of recruiting system simply couldn't exist in Idaho, Arizona, or Wyoming. Institutions like these have always been plagued by problems related to location. Such teams may peak occasionally, but they have great difficulty in sustaining excellence from one season to the next.

Another factor affecting conference success is the degree of local recruiting intensity. This is a function of the number of universities in a given area attempting to field big-time athletic teams relative to the available supply of high caliber athletes. When intense intrastate competition exists, one of the universities usually dominates. Through the years, Alabama has outclassed Auburn, Illinois has gotten the best of Northwestern, Oklahoma has dominated Oklahoma State, Kansas has held forth over Kansas State, and Tennessee has won out over Vanderbilt. The conferences

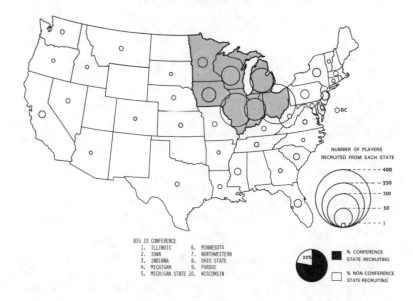

Figure 34. Big 10 Conference recruiting (data base: 1980 rosters).

selected for analysis here are illustrative of an extreme range in recruiting behavior.

The Big Ten

The Big Ten (figure 34) is comprised of ten universities from seven relatively populous states: Wisconsin, Minnesota, Ohio, Indiana, Michigan, Illinois, and Iowa. Wisconsin and Minnesota each have only one big-time football program; Ohio State is by far the dominant university in Ohio; and Michigan, Iowa and Illinois support but two standouts each. Indiana, with Purdue, Indiana, and independent Notre Dame, is the only Big Ten state that rates as an overemphasizer (because there just isn't that much high school football talent there).

Big Ten conference members *should* (and probably would if not for relaxed academic entrance standards in surrounding regions) be able to tap their respective states' best, filling out their rosters from the Illinois-Ohio surplus and from nearby Pennsylvania. We have seen, however, that even this kind of advantage cannot insure success in today's athletic talent market.

The Big Ten confines most of its recruiting activity to the member states, which contain a great many potential footballers. Illinois and Ohio, though, comprise the most fertile supply areas, together staffing nearly one-half of the conference rosters. On average, 40 percent of the conference recruiting is done out of state. Purdue, Iowa, and Northwestern are most dependent on imported players, especially from Illinois and Ohio. Pennsylvania is the only significant source from outside the conference region.

The Western Athletic

The Big Ten has a considerable edge over the up-and-coming Western Athletic Conference (figure 35). The WAC is comprised of universities from the sparsely populated West. Member institutions include Wyoming, Air Force, Colorado State, New Mexico, Texas–El Paso, Utah, Brigham Young, Hawaii, and San Diego State. Seven of the universities face intense recruiting competition from other schools within their home states. And with the exception of Texas, none of the member states are significant suppliers of athletic talent. As a result, the WAC recruits 67 percent of its players from outside the conference boundaries. California, Pennsylvania, and Illinois are the major suppliers, but no area is left untouched by the gypsy talent-seekers, who tap players from all available sources.

Southwest

A few of the major conferences are essentially one-state organiza-

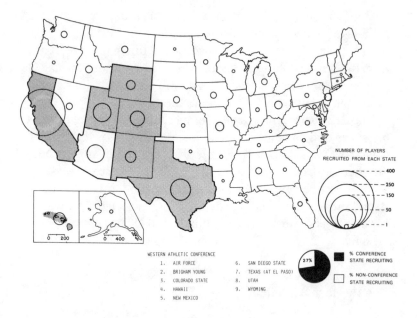

Figure 35. Western Athletic Conference recruiting (data base: 1980 rosters).

tions. The Southwest Conference is primarily a Texas affair, and even though the state is the "Holy Land of high school football" it has been unable to provide enough outstanding talent for conference members. During the 1960s and early 1970s, the conference was dominated by the University of Texas. But enough good teams have been assembled at Texas A & M, SMU, Rice, TCU, Baylor and neighboring Arkansas to keep things interesting. Since Houston's admission to the conference and SMU's resurgence, the University of Texas's supremacy has been severely challenged. Still, the Longhorn-Royal-Akers recruiting systems have been undeniably superior to those of the competition, probably because of the UT alumni network and the winning tradition that pervades every facet of the program.

Pac Ten

In recent years the Pacific Ten (figure 36) has become a California phenomenon. The conference has been controlled by USC and UCLA, with occasional rumblings from Stanford, Cal, and the out-of-state contingent. The California dominance also applies to the player supply characteristics of the organization. California athletes comprise 95 percent of the in-state total and well over half of the Oregon and Washington rosters. The trend has been for the Los Angeles schools to scrap for southern California's best, leaving the others to pick up what is left.

The SEC

The Southeastern Conference relies almost exclusively on home-grown football players (figure 37). Only 33 percent of the players were out-of-state recruits and just 12 percent hailed from states located outside the conference. Kentucky and Vanderbilt, perennial second-division finishers, were the only universities to obtain more than half of their players from outside their respective states. Florida and Georgia were heavily recruited by other conference members, together supplying nearly one-third of the total conference needs. Recruiting outside the conference area was extremely spotty. South Carolina and Ohio were the only states tapped for more than a handful of players.

The ACC

The Atlantic Coast Conference, consisting of the South Atlantic states of North and South Carolina, Virginia, and Maryland, operates in marked contrast to its neighbor, the Southeastern Conference (figure 38). Nearly half of the Atlantic Coast Conference footballers are lured to the area from non-conference states, and

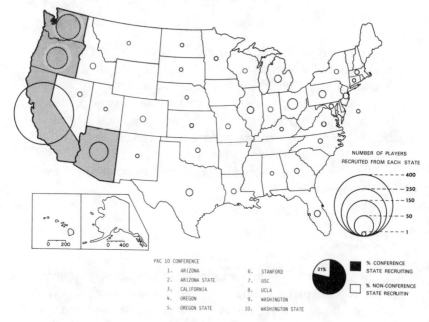

Figure 36. Pacific 10 Conference recruiting (data base: 1980 rosters).

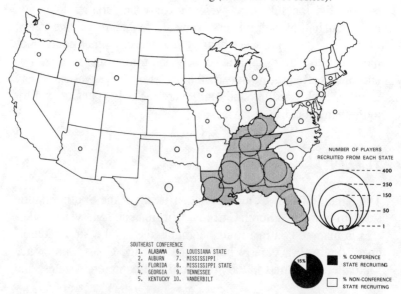

Figure 37. Southeastern Conference recruiting (data base: 1980 rosters).

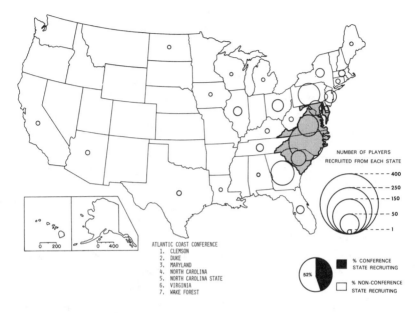

Figure 38. Atlantic Coast Conference recruiting (data base: 1980 rosters).

less than 40 percent of the recruits compete at schools in their home states.

Only North Carolina and Wake Forest recruit the majority of their players from the home state. Maryland, Virginia, and Duke obtain only 25 percent of their talent at home. The reliance on out-of-state players is so great that Pennsylvania and New Jersey provide more players than three of the four conference member states (Maryland, Virginia, and South Carolina) combined. The conference also depends heavily on Ohio, New York, Georgia, and Illinois. In short, the Atlantic Coast Conference could not compete in big-time football circles without a substantial infusion of outside talent, and even with extensive importation, many of its schools are struggling.

The conference is also dependent on outside suppliers for its basketball programs. Though since fewer athletes are required, the membership has done very well in that department. In the case of basketball, the combination of local talent with that imported from New York, New Jersey, Ohio, Pennsylvania, and Indiana has made the Atlantic Coast Conference one of the outstanding conferences. But again we see the necessity of a local supply pool for the maintenance of a consistently high-quality football program. The Atlantic Coast Conference has the worst of both worlds — too many universities compete for talent in a small area that produces a severely limited number of quality football players.

The Big Eight

The Big Eight's success is an outgrowth of an aggressive nationally based recruiting thrust (figure 39). Missouri is the lone member institution which relies on the home area for the bulk of its football players. Just 52 percent of the conference players are drawn from the states which comprise the conference region.

The strategy is to get the best local boys first and then to round up the players who can contribute to a winning program, regardless of where they are from. As a result, the conference has more Texans, Illinoisans, and Californians than it does Iowans, Nebraskans, or Coloradans. The Oklahoma schools have a Texas flavor, while Colorado and Nebraska have relied heavily on California. The Kansas schools, Missouri, and Iowa State are partial to Illinois and states to the east.

The Missouri Valley and the Big Sky

The Missouri Valley and Big Sky conferences are not particularly noted for their football prowess (figures 40 and 41). The universities which comprise their membership, however, carry on sophisticated and expensive national recruiting programs. West Texas State is the only school in either conference located in the midst of an ample supply of quality football talent. Three members of the Big Sky are located in Idaho and two are in Montana. It is doubtful

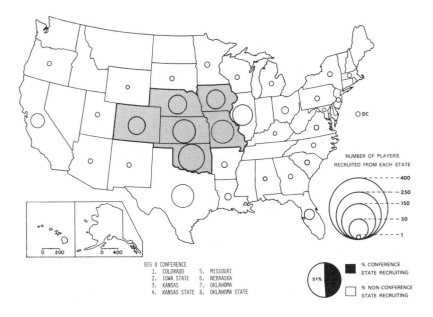

Figure 39. Big 8 Conference recruiting (data base: 1980 rosters).

that the two states combined could consistently produce enough quality players to man just one first-class college team. As a result, the Big Sky imports nearly 60 percent of its players from outside the conference region. California and Washington are the biggest donors, but there is considerable dependence on Illinois, Ohio, Massachusetts, and New York.

Most of the Missouri Valley universities must play second or third fiddle to other universities in their respective states. Wichita State is a poor football cousin to Kansas and Kansas State, Tulsa to Oklahoma and frequently to Oklahoma State, Drake to Iowa and Iowa State, Illinois State to Illinois, and so on.

Nevertheless, each of the Missouri Valley institutions (excepting Drake) appears committed to upgrading the stature of its football team. And since most of them have difficulty competing with their in-state rivals for the prime local talent, they must expand their search to other areas. Most of the Missouri Valley and Big

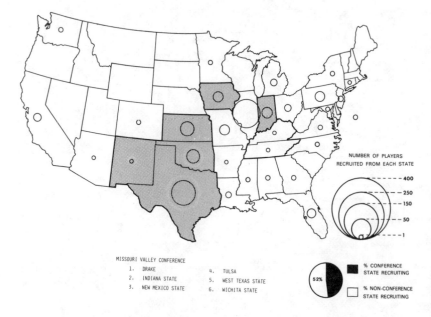

Figure 40. Missouri Valley Conference recruiting (data base: 1980 rosters).
Note: Although a conference member, St. Louis University does not play football.

Sky members fish the big talent ponds and keep whatever they can catch. As a group they are either giving big-time football a go without access to an adequate local supply of players or competing in the shadow of established and tradition-laden institutions.

The Ivy League

The Ivy League is unique among the major athletic conferences (figure 42). It claims a rich past, having dominated collegiate football during the cradle years and later helping to diffuse it to points west and south by engaging in the first intersectional competition. The glory days are past, for the league operates under an arrangement which prohibits athletic scholarships, out-of-season practice, intersectional competition, and postseason games.

Ivy League schools still recruit athletes, but most of those who win scholarships must do so on the merits of their academic ability. As a result, Ivy League football players reflect the geographic distribution of the general student population more closely than players at any of the other conferences. Of the league's players, 74% come from outside the state in which their school is located, and if it were not for Penn and Harvard, which rely heavily on Pennsylvania and Massachusetts respectively, the figure would approach 90 percent.

At the extreme, over a recent four-year span, Dartmouth and Brown obtained only one player each from New Hampshire and Rhode Island. But even though the Ivy League contingent is a cosmopolitan lot, over 60 percent of the players are from states represented in the Ivy League. In fact, over one-half of the footballers come from four states; Pennsylvania, New York, New Jersey, and Massachusetts. Ohio and Illinois are the chief foreign sources.

Conference Recruitment of Future Professional Players

The ultimate goal of most elite college football players is to move up to the National Football League. Thus, by examining collegiate recruitment of those who are good enough to become professionals, we are able to comprehend the national emphasis that now characterizes the recruiting game. Prof. Bill Turner, of the Clark University graduate school of geography, has conducted research on the high school origins and collegiate origins of NFL players.[1] His maps demonstrate substantial contrasts among some of the major athletic conferences (figures 43, 44, and 45). For example, the Big Ten obtained the majority of its future professionals from within the conference region; however, the percentage of players coming from out-of-conference states was considerably higher (over 30 percent) among those who made it to the pros than among

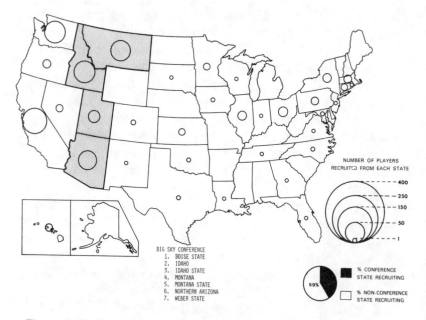

Figure 41. Big Sky Conference recruiting (data base: 1980 rosters).

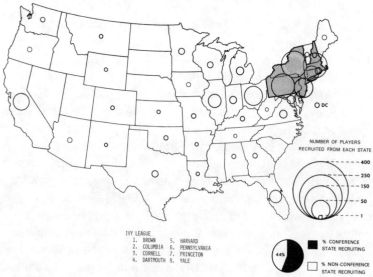

Figure 42. Ivy League recruiting (data base: 1980 rosters).

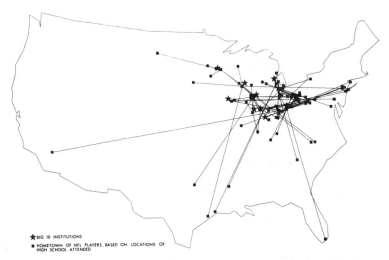

Figure 43. Origins of NFL players who attended Big 10 institutions (data base: 1977 NFL rosters, compiled by Bill Turner).

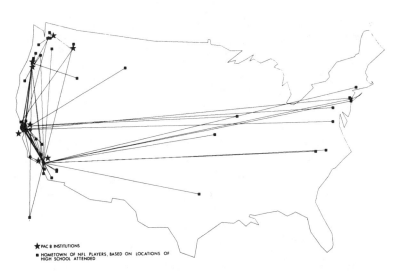

Figure 44. Origins of NFL players who attended Pacific 10 institutions (data base: 1977 NFL rosters, compiled by Bill Turner).

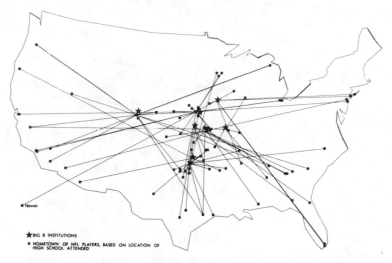

Figure 45. Origins of NFL players who attended Big 8 institutions (data base: 1977 NFL rosters, compiled by Bill Turner).

those who did not. The same circumstance prevailed in the Pacific Ten (the Pacific Eight at the time of the study), which recruited 92 percent of its players from member states. While only 8% of all players came from outside the conference, nearly 26 percent of the best players were recruited from other parts of the country. Finally, the Big Eight map forcefully conveys the importance of national recruiting. The conference has prospered on its ability to bring in the unusually talented, regardless of location.

Conference recruiting territories have evolved over long time spans. They reflect the territorial ideas of member coaches and the quality of local and regional schoolboy competition. Each coach has his own contacts and scouting network; players and professional associates, alumni, and black-market flesh-peddlers. Typically, the first step is to comb the immediate region, and, depending on population density and the quality of play, this may take care of much of the demand. In addition, agreements with small colleges with regard to local prospects are not uncommon.

The recruiting strategies of any university are subject to change. A new coach, territorial raids by other coaches, and improvement in high school programs are all important factors in the process of change. As a result, the geography of recruiting is extremely dynamic, as coaches are hired and fired, as new universities opt for big-time football, as conferences and scholastic requirements for athletes are altered, as redshirting rules are changed, and as the football fortunes of universities rise and fall.

8
The National Dimensions of Basketball Recruiting

The regional surplus-deficit patterns (figure 46), combined with the basketball reputation that places like New York City, Philadelphia, Washington, D.C., and the region (Illinois, Indiana, Kentucky) referred to as IllInKy have come to enjoy, have resulted in massive movements of talent across the United States.[1] New Yorkers are going to Kansas, Illinoisans to Texas, Hoosiers to Mississippi, Californians to Utah, and so on and on. As is the case with football, high-pressure national recruiting has become essential to big-time basketball.

The IllInKy Surplus

From an interregional viewpoint, two extensive recruitment flows can be identified (figure 47). The most imposing originates in Illinois, Indiana, and Kentucky, the IllInKy region, and streams to a total of forty-two states. The Midwest, the Deep South, Texas, and the Atlantic Coast are the prime benefactors. In addition, a sub-

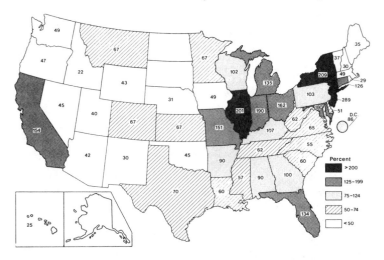

Figure 46. State surplus and deficits of big time collegiate basketball talent (data base: 1971–77 rosters). Numbers indicate the percentage of its own needs supplied by each state.

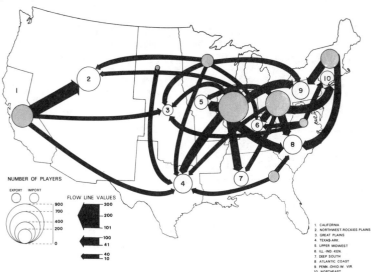

Figure 47. Interregional migrant behavior of college-bound basketball players (major colleges) (data base: 1971–72, 1976–77, 1980–81 rosters).

135

Table 10: Leading Exporters of Basketball Talent, 1969–81

Rank	State	Total Production	Exports	Percent Exported
1	New York	1187	693	58
2	Illinois	1033	664	64
3	California	1297	572	44
4	New Jerscy	672	532	80
5	Pennsylvania	897	494	55
6	Indiana	727	488	67
7	Ohio	893	465	51
8	Kentucky	436	264	61
9	Michigan	481	222	46

stantial number of players are also cajoled and lured to the Great Plains and the Rocky Mountain zone.

This exodus of roundballers is a measure of the esteem in which IllInKy basketball is held by college coaches and recruiters around the country and reflects a breeding capacity which greatly exceeds local consumption. Many of the best prospects have been recruited great distances from IllInKy at considerable expense to the universities involved—and to the detriment of the area's own collegiate programs. The decline in the 1960s of formerly good basketball schools like Illinois, Indiana, Northwestern, Purdue, and Notre Dame, accompanied by the rise of obscure (where basketball was concerned) schools like New Mexico, Jacksonville, Mississippi State, Texas Western (UTEP), Houston, Southwestern Louisiana, and Tennessee provides ample testimony: a lot of the best boys were getting away (table 10).

This situation has resulted in a more intensive effort by the local coaches, which has already paid dividends for Bobby Knight at Indiana, Bob King and Bill Hodges at Indiana State, Digger Phelps at Notre Dame, Lew Henson at Illinois, and George King and Lee Rose at Purdue. Knight has become particularly adept at selling Indiana University to the types of Hoosier hotshots who were leaving the state with predictable regularity. Indiana State has also developed a first-class program by utilizing a similar strategy.

The extent to which the basketball heartland is combed by the talent hustlers is illustrated by the fact that nearly every serious basketball school has at least one IllInKy player on its squad. The overnight success stories of the many collegiate basketball newcomers who have staffed their teams from this area provide unmistakable evidence regarding the geographic impact of the region. Without Illinois and Indiana to draw on while waiting for their high school programs to catch up, it is doubtful that universities from Michigan, Wisconsin, Tennessee, Texas, and the states of the Deep South would have been able to field respectable big-time teams.

Players from IllInKy have helped to elevate competition in all parts of the country. Their diffusion has probably been the most significant geographical force in the national development of high-quality basketball. The list of institutions that have made it with IllInKy talent is too long to recount here, but Houston is a good example. In 1965, its first outstanding basketball year, the Houston roster contained eight players from IllInKy and only two from Texas. The team that finished second to UCLA in 1967 had only one Texan. The emergence of the University of Texas at El Paso followed much the same pattern. New Mexico and New Mexico State University regularly obtain their players from Illinois and Indiana, and there are many others. Before Waymon Tisdale, Oklahoma's recent rise had been underwritten almost entirely by Indiana and Ohio boys.

The gradual emergence of quality high school basketball in the Southeast has been the result of a diffusion process originating in IllInKy. Exposure to first-rate, imported college basketball has had a great impact on the high schools, particularly in the region's urban areas. If the trend continued (and it will, according to my twenty-one-year sampling of recruiting), the South will eventually be self-sufficient in the basketball department, its players and coaches having learned the game from IllInKy imports.

I questioned numerous high school coaches in the IllInKy region about the collegiate recruiting effort there. All of them believed that the *world's best* high school basketball was played in Illinois, Indiana, and Kentucky. A few volunteered that a "quality" game was also played in Ohio, the New York–New Jersey area, and "around Philadelphia and Washington, D.C." This opinion was, of course, largely derived from written accounts in the popular press and from the occasional appearance of a boy from one of those areas on a local university team.

One coach from a small consolidated school in Southern Indiana expressed it this way:

Yes I do feel that Indiana basketball ranks at the top, or near the top, in relation to other states. I am probably biased in this respect, but my thinking on the matter has become stronger the past few years. I say this because, time after time, I receive mail from college coaches begging for Indiana basketball players. Just yesterday, a good-sized college in Minnesota called me and outright told me that they had to recruit some Indiana boys or their future in basketball would be dim. Of course, this is one case, but it has happened time after time.[2]

The head coach from Shelbyville, Indiana, was more succinct: "Other states have good teams and players, but not as many as Indiana."[3] The feeling of basketball superiority is equally strong in Illinois, as these comments from Elgin indicate: "The best basketball is played in northern Illinois and New York City. Elgin is a great basketball town, like others in this area including Rockford, Freeport, Lasalle-Peru, Joliet and Aurora. I have sent 65 Elgin boys on to college ball since 1950."[4] Even the Utah high school coaches stated that the interscholastic game reached its zenith in IllInKy.

Within the region, Illinois is the leading exporter, ranking second nationally (table 10). Indiana ranks sixth, and both states have similar export patterns (figures 48 and 49). Illinois is a more significant supplier for midwestern universities, particularly those in Iowa, Michigan, Missouri, and Kansas, while Hoosiers tend to be more important to Florida and Ohio. Both states are major feed-

Figure 48. Migration of Illinois high school basketball players to major colleges (data base: 1971–72, 1976–77, 1980–81 rosters).

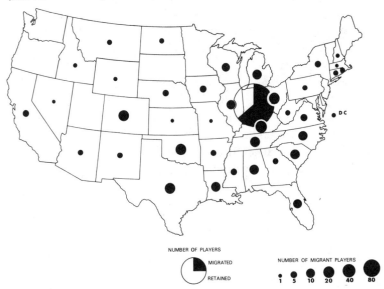

Figure 49. Migration of Indiana high school basketball players to major colleges (data base: 1971–72, 1976–77, 1980–81 rosters).

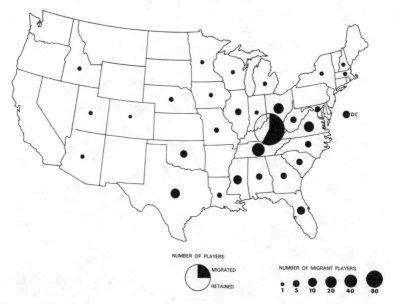

Figure 50. Migration of Kentucky high school basketball players to major colleges (data base: 1971–72, 1976–77, 1980–81 rosters).

ers for programs in Texas and Colorado. Together they have contributed to the basketball success of nearly every major college in the United States.

The region's southern member, Kentucky, has made its impact primarily in the Deep South. The presence of the late Adolph Rupp at the University of Kentucky was the most important geographical factor in the development of southern basketball. His unparalleled success pressed the southern schools to improve their basketball programs, largely by recruiting high school players from his state and from the Ohio Valley region (figure 50).

THE PENNSYLVANIA–OHIO SURPLUS

A second impressive flow of hoopsters streams out from Pennsylvania and Ohio (figures 51 and 52), states that rank fifth and seventh respectively in the export ratings (table 10). This surplus

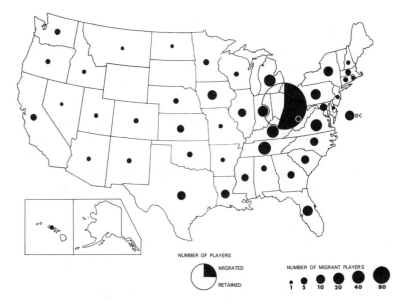

Figure 51. Migration of Ohio high school basketball players to major colleges (data base: 1971–72, 1976–77, 1980–81 rosters).

Figure 52. Migration of Pennsylvania high school basketball players to major colleges (data base: 1971–72, 1976–77, 1980–81 rosters).

of basketball skills has been attracted primarily by the Atlantic Coast and Southeastern Conference schools. A number of northeastern universities have also recruited the area. The Atlantic Coast region consumes 17 percent of the exports, and the Northeast 22 percent. The Ohio flow has a strong southerly component, whereas Pennsylvania hoopsters, like those from IllInKy, have been in greater demand out west. In total, forty-four states recruited from the region. The rosters at perennial stalwarts like Duke, Maryland, North Carolina, North Carolina State, and Wake Forest are generously sprinkled with Pennsylvania and Ohio products.

Most of the Pennsylvania hoopsters who migrate to the Northeast attend college in New York or New Jersey. The group includes a high percentage of boys from the Philadelphia area. This movement is partly offset by the flow of New Jerseyites into Pennsylvania, a phenomenon indicative of the local recruiting intensity within the megalopolitan zone stretching from New York City to Washington, D.C.

RECRUITING FROM THE NORTHEAST

The northeastern region is one of limited surplus, with the export pool confined almost entirely to New York and New Jersey (figures 53 and 54), states which rank first and fourth nationally as exporters of players. New Jersey sends out many more boys than it takes in because the state provides only limited opportunities for the utilization of their talents. New York, on the other hand, is a major importer. Over 40 percent of the two states' exports stay in the Northeast, and of those who leave, nearly half journey no farther than Pennsylvania or the adjacent Atlantic Coast region. The rapid emergence of the Big East conference, led by Georgetown, Villanova, Syracuse, and Boston College, has resulted almost exclusively from recruitment of talent within the conference region. It is apparent that most eastern seaboard coaches regard the entire northeastern territory as their own. The migratory behavior of northeastern hoopsters is, in many ways, analogous to that of

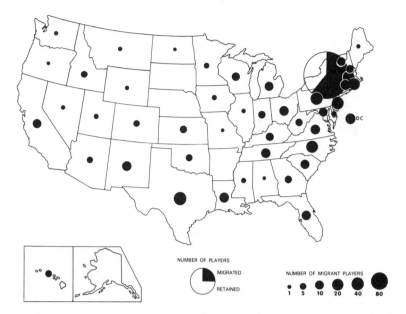

Figure 53. Migration of New York high school basketball players to major colleges (data base: 1971–72, 1976–77, 1980–81 rosters).

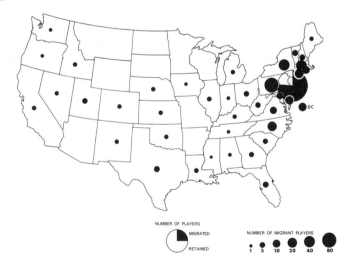

Figure 54. Migration of New Jersey high school basketball players to major colleges (data base: 1971–72, 1976–77, 1980–81 rosters).

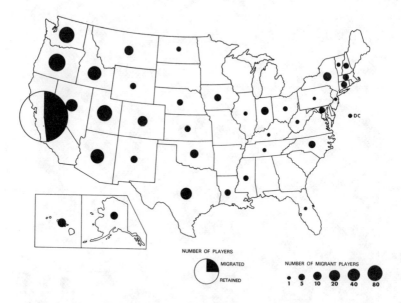

Figure 55. Migration of California high school basketball players to major colleges (data base: 1971–72, 1976–77, 1980–81 rosters).

Texas footballers. The Northeast has its own style of play and takes great pride in what Pete Axthelm has labeled the "city game."[5] Hence, most of the eastern powers are manned by local products.

The demand for northeastern players is becoming more widespread, though, as the rush to Texas indicates. There are even trickles toward the Midwest and the Southeast. In recent years Marquette and UCLA have utilized New York and New Jersey talent to considerable advantage, and the University of South Carolina, long the doormat of the Atlantic Coast conference, sprang forth as an independent basketball power through the almost exclusive use of New York products.

CALIFORNIA

California, the third leading exporter of hardwood talent, is a prin-

144

cipal donor to universities in the Northwest, in Texas, and in some sections of the Rocky Mountain zone (figure 55). Oregon, Utah, Washington, and Arizona are the major recipients. Californians have supplemented the local talent in Utah, Idaho, and Oregon, helping to build several nationally ranked contenders in these states. A few of these teams of California rejects have been good enough to upset UCLA, helping to put an end to the dynasty forged by John Wooden and his successors. Although many players from California have been drawn to locations as far east as Colorado and Oklahoma, they have not yet become a force in the IllInKy heartland. The basketball and football migrations from California are remarkably similar. In both sports, the state serves the talent needs of the Pacific Coast and Western Athletic conferences. Most schools in this area are also dependent on the IllInKy and Midwest areas.

GENERAL PATTERNS

The outstanding high school basketball players are sought out regardless of where they live and, like their football counterparts, are often beseiged by more offers than they can realistically consider. New York City and environs, Philadelphia, Washington, D.C., Detroit, Pittsburgh, Chicago, and Los Angeles are the hunting grounds of most serious recruiters. In these seven cities, the talent seekers could have observed over one-quarter of the major college players recruited since 1961. Some of the best players are veterans of the rigorous competition associated with high schools of multi-thousand enrollments, as well as of years of ghetto playground experience, and the fact that they perform in the shadow of numerous city universities, coaches, asphalt hustlers, and scouts greatly enhances the probability of their being recruited. In addition, the presence of alumni from an array of colleges helps to insure that they will not be overlooked. The city-gamers have spelled success for schools as far apart as UCLA and South Carolina. Most of them, however, perform locally, where opportunity abounds. As a result, teams like Villanova, Georgetown, Providence, Manhat-

145

tan, St. John's, La Salle, St. Joseph's, Iona, Pennsylvania, Rutgers, Princeton, Syracuse, Boston College, and Columbia regularly field strong entries.

Fierce competition for the well-known high school stalwarts in a given area is to be expected. But there is also a substantial movement of the journeyman prepsters across state and regional boundaries. Over 60 percent of the major college players participate outside their home state, and 35 percent cross over the broad regional divisions which were previously identified.

9
Cheating

The overzealous pursuit of football and basketball excellence has fostered a fast and lose attitude toward the so-called amateur code. Recruiting and excessive aid violations are commonplace. Many of the prestigious athletic programs associated with some of the outstanding universities in the United States have been found guilty of infractions and sentenced to multi-year probations. And, sadly for collegiate sport, the known offenders represent only a small percentage of the actual culprits.

No one knows the precise magnitude of the cheating. A study made in 1976 by the national coaches' committee on recruiting concluded that *only* 12 percent of the schools cheat.[1] But according to Frank Arnold, chairman of the committee, "those 12 percent reach 40 percent of the players." In 1984, Walter Byers, the NCAA executive director, said that 30 percent of the Division 1 schools were cheating. According to Byers, "There seems to be a growing number of coaches and administrators who look upon NCAA penalties as the price of doing business—if you get punished that's unfortunate, but that's part of the cost of getting along."[2]

The southwestern experiences of Billy Brooks, a former wide receiver with the Cincinnati Bengals, who attended Oklahoma University, led him to believe that everybody cheats. In an interview with Danny Robbins of the *Austin American-Statesman*, Brooks described some of his own experiences: "SMU told me they could pull strings and get me in, but there'd always be the chance somebody would find out. So I went to [Navarro] junior college one year, finished with a 3.85 [grade-point average] and went to OU." Once at Oklahoma, he received special treatment, including a free leather coat at a clothing store operated by an Oklahoma fan, a free watch-repair job at a jewelry store run by another OU booster, and a car loan on which he had to pay only $60 every two months.

Brooks said he never felt guilty about accepting gifts, particularly the coat. "I needed a coat. That was the extent of my concern." Brooks also said he bought up books of season tickets and sold them for enormous profits, but he refused to say how much.

Although Texas recruited Brooks, he said that Texas "talked to me like I was a little black boy with no other place to go. Texas didn't really offer me anything illegal, they just talked to me in terms of certain advantages of going to Texas. Money? A car? A degree? I can't pinpoint it. But at the time I was a poor black guy from the east side of Austin. I thought in terms of bucks." Brooks believes that his experience was not uncommon: "I'm out of school now; I don't want to make waves. But shoot, let's face it. Everybody cheats. All colleges in my opinion are illegally recruiting. That's Oklahoma, that's Texas, that's everybody. There are just too many rules in that book. It's easy to break one."[3]

The Jerry Eckwood case serves as an example of how far the cheaters will go to attain success. Bob Hattibaugh, Eckwood's high school coach in Brinkley, Arkansas, described it as follows:

He could have driven off in anything from a VW to a Caddy. One alumnus wanted to give Jerry $500 a month to attend his school. Jerry kidded him and said he needed more. The guy came back the next day and said, "I got it up to $1000." That was from an Arkansas booster before Jerry got interested in the Razorbacks. [He eventually signed with them.] He was offered $1500 a month to work for a record company as a salesman. Another alumnus said he would fix him up with a $2500 a month job and all the cars he needed. One school said they would buy his mother a new home, get his girl a scholarship, give him a car, and a $1000 a month summer job in addition to his scholarship. After hearing that, other schools came in and tried to top the offer.[4]

In his report to the American Council on Education, *A National Study of Intercollegiate Athletics,* George Hanford stated: "External competition from professional sports, selective treatment by the media, as well as pressure from alumni and the public have put big time collegiate athletic programs into competition with each other, not only on the playing field, but in the market for entertainers/performers/athletes."[5] The conclusion sounds like a repeat of the 1929 Carnegie report. A cleansing of collegiate athletics was called for years ago, but rather than improving, things have grown steadily worse.

According to the American Council on Education study, the need to win on the field has led to a myriad of ethical problems related to recruiting, financial subsidies, and the on-campus care and feeding of college athletes. The study points out some of the recruiting violations which came to the attention of the inquiry team. The following is just a partial list:

— altering high school academic transcripts
— threatening to bomb the home of a high school principal who refused to alter transcripts
— changing admissions test scores
— having substitutes, including assistant coaches, take admissions tests
— offering jobs to parents or other relatives of a prospect
— promising one package of financial aid and delivering another
— firing from a state job the father of a prospect who enrolled at other than that state's university
— "tipping" or otherwise paying athletes who perform particularly well on a given occasion— and then on subsequent ones
— providing a community college basketball star with a private apartment and a car

— providing a quarterback with a new car every year, his favorite end with a "tip," and the interior linemen with nothing
— getting grades for athletes in courses they never attended
— enrolling university big-time athletes in junior colleges out-of-season and getting them grades there for courses they never attended
— using federal work-study funds to pay athletes for questionable or nonexistent jobs
— getting a portion of the work-study funds paid to athletes "kicked back" into the athletic department kitty
— forcing injured players to "get back in the game"

The study of Southwestern Louisiana University is illustrative of the kind of blatant cheating that has occurred. Partially accounting for the university's rapid surge to the top of the intercollegiate basketball ranks were the following violations: recruitment of one blue-chip prospect with a promise of a full scholarship, $450 a month, free clothing, free air travel for himself and his parents, free laundry, free transportation to the campus for registration, and a substitute to take his scholastic aptitude test; erroneous certification of academic eligibility; free long-distance telephone privileges and free air transportation home for a number of players; purchase of poker chips in a gambling casino for player use.[6]

Hanford volunteered no estimate concerning the number of these and other types of violations. He deplored the fact that the majority of the college powers continually reject any move toward de-emphasis, particularly in regard to the need issue. Suggestions for the adoption of a grant-in-aid, or need, program instead of full scholarships, for elimination of spring practice, for a limited substitution rule, and for scholarship reduction have all met with stubborn resistance.

The need question was put to a vote at each NCAA national convention between 1973 and 1979. It failed to pass, except at the Division III — small school — level. The proposals have called for the abolition of full-ride grants-in-aid. Full rides would be replaced by financial awards to student athletes on the basis of need.

Those who favor the need approach point out that need awards

Table 11: Categories for NCAA Probations, 1952–76

Violations	Number of Occurrences
Recruiting	75
Improper aid	36
Funds	20
Admitting athletes who did not predict a 1.6 grade point	13
Uncertified game	13
Out-of-season practice	9
Ethics	6
Using ineligible players	5
Extra benefits	4
Improper administration	4
Improper admission	3
Ineligible player	2
Membership obligations	2
Outside aid	1
Financial aid	1
Excess aid	1
Academic standards	1

are standard practice with those students who do not participate in intercollegiate athletics. In addition to solving the problem of special treatment to athletes, awards based on need would also save money, perhaps as much as $250,000 per institution annually. So why hasn't it passed? The case against adopting a need policy hinges on the argument that such a policy would result in *increased* under-the-table payments to athletes. The belief is that coaches are under so much pressure that they would exceed the need formula, and that athletes would accept the awards. And that assessment is probably correct.

A return to a need system would be a major step toward putting intercollegiate athletes back into perspective. Fritz Crisler, whose observation in 1937 concerning athletic scholarships was quoted in chapter two, was back on the podium in 1956. Speaking with Herman Hickman, the noted Yale coach and football commentator, Crisler put the case bluntly: ''We have discarded the principles on which college football was established . . . we are applying professional tactics to educational ideals and college athletics. We are very aggressive in scouting and recruiting, and we offer arrangements bordering on a paid-player basis. . . . We are nourishing a monster which can destroy us if we admit we are powerless to resist or control it."[7] He went on to say that athletes should seek colleges just as other students do and that all recruiting should be stopped.

What has resulted from the policies of recent decades? The evidence suggests that cheating is acceptable behavior. From 1952 to 1985 the NCAA placed over 150 schools on either football or basketball probation. The majority of violations consisted of illegal recruiting practices, misuse of athletic funds, or improper aid to athletes (tables 11 and 12). In all fairness it should be pointed out that the NCAA is both judge and jury, and that when the organization convicts a school, there is no appeal process. On the other hand, the NCAA investigates only those schools against which a complaint has been filed.

Football and basketball cheating shows a regional pattern (figures 56 and 57) that conforms to regional recruiting intensity. Football cheating tends to be most concentrated in Texas, Oklahoma, Kansas, and the Southeast, the areas dominated by the Big Eight, Southwest, and Southeastern conferences. The basketball culprits are concentrated in the Carolinas, Florida, Kentucky, Illinois, Louisiana, and Kansas. The patterns are suggestive of a relationship between the overzealous pursuit of excellence and cheating.

Probation apparently has little effect upon the success of the sanctioned sports at the universities involved. In fact, cheating has paid rich dividends for many. Most of the penalized schools continued to be big winners in the sport involved. North Carolina State was placed on probation for the recruitment of David Thompson. Following a one-year ban from postseason competition, the Wolfpack came back in 1974 to capture the national title. The team's most valuable player was, of course, David Thompson.

Oklahoma won the Associated Press national football crown

Table 12: Recent NCAA Sanctions

University	Dates of Probation	Sport	Sanctions	Grounds for Probation
Akron	9/84– 9/86	Men's basket-ball	No postseason competition in 1984–85 academic year; two scholarships cut in 1985–86.	Illegal benefits to athletes, improper recruiting.
Alabama State	5/85– 12/86	Football	Head coach excluded from recruiting for one year.	Use of ineligible players.
Alaska (Anchorage)	5/84– 5/86	Men's basket-ball	Two scholarships cut in 1984–85.	Illegal benefits to athletes, improper recruiting.
Arizona	5/83– 5/85	Football	No postseason competition in 1983 and 1984; no televised games in 1984–85 and 1985–86.	Illegal benefits to athletes, improper recruiting, maintaining slush fund.
Arizona State	12/84– 12/86	Baseball, men's gymnastics, and wrestling	No postseason competition in 1984–85; forfeiture of 1984 Pacific 10 Conference championship in baseball; scholarships reduced in all three sports.	Illegal benefits to athletes.

Table 12: Recent NCAA Sanctions (*continued*)

University	Dates of Probation	Sport	Sanctions	Grounds for Probation
Florida	1/85– 1/88	Football	No postseason competition in 1984–85 and 1985–86; no televised games in 1985–86 and 1986–87; football scholarships reduced from 95 to 85 in 1985–86 and to 75 in 1986–87.	Illegal benefits to athletes, improper recruiting, scouting violations.
Georgia	1/85– 5/86	Men's basketball and football	Basketball: revenues ($254,880) from 1984–85 tournament recalled; coaches barred from off-campus recruiting for one year. Football: scholarships cut from 30 to 23 in 1985–86 and 1986–87; three boosters excluded from program.	Illegal benefits to athletes, improper recruiting.
Illinois	7/84– 7/86	Football	No postseason competition in 1984–85; no televised	Illegal benefits to athletes, improper

School	Dates	Sport	Penalties	Violations
Illinois (*continued*)			games in 1985–86 regular season; no off-campus recruiting by football coaches.	recruiting, unethical conduct.
Kansas	11/83–11/85	Football	No postseason competition or televised games in 1984–85.	Illegal benefits to athletes, improper recruiting, eligibility violations.
USC	4/82–4/85	Football	No postseason competition in 1982–83 and 1983–84; no televised games in 1983–84 and 1985–86; one coach prohibited from recruiting for two years, sixteen boosters excluded from program.	Illegal benefits to athletes, admissions violations.
Southern Mississippi	2/85–2/86	Football	Paid on-campus visits by prospective recruits cut from 95 to 60; no televised games in 1985–86 (suspended).	Illegal benefits to athletes, improper recruiting.
Tennessee State	2/85–2/86	Football	Revenues ($80,052.80) from 1981 and 1982 Division I-AA	Eligibility violations in football, baseball,

155

Table 12: Recent NCAA Sanctions (*continued*)

University	Dates of Probation	Sport	Sanctions	Grounds for Probation
Tennessee State (*continued*)			championships recalled; record of participation deleted; no postseason competition in 1985–86 (suspended).	men's and women's basketball, swimming, and men's track and field
Wisconsin (Madison)	11/83– 11/84	Football	No televised games in 1985–86; one athletic representative excluded from recruiting.	Improper recruiting.
SMU		Football	Loss of 45 scholarships; no televised games in 1986; no postseason competition in 1985–86.	Illegal benefits to athletes, improper recruiting.

Figure 56. NCAA probationary actions: football, 1952–84.

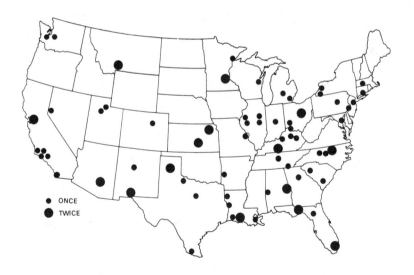

Figure 57. NCAA probationary actions: basketball, 1952–84.

while on probation. The penalty followed upon the actions of several Sooners who had conspired to alter the high school transcript of quarterback Kerry Jackson. Head football coach Barry Switzer, however, was able to play on the sympathies of Oklahoma boosters to turn the probation into a fund-raising and recruiting bonanza. The 1984–85 Florida response to sanctions has been a clone of the Sooner reaction. The fans, boosters, and administration behaved as though nothing had happened.

The cheating disease continued to spread. Since 1977 a growing number of the big-name schools have been caught and punished for improper recruiting and illegal payments to athletes. USC, UCLA, Florida, Clemson, SMU, Oklahoma State, Illinois, Kansas, Georgia, Wisconsin, Arizona, and Arizona State, a group of first-class academic institutions, have been tarnished by their athletic indiscretions. Most recently, Texas Christian University has admitted that its top football players were being paid to play. Worse yet, the payment scheme was coordinated by a member of the TCU board of trustees.

The Florida, SMU, and TCU cases are representative of the growing malaise. Florida and SMU relied heavily on the illegal recruitment and the payment of players to develop their all-time best teams. The 1984 Florida team won the Southeastern Conference and was ranked number one in the country by several polls that chose to ignore their probationary status. And despite a severe reduction in the number of football scholarships the 1985 team was a big winner, attaining the number-one ranking on November 4. Despite a three-year probation including a loss of twenty scholarships, and a two-year ban on television and postseason competition, Gator fans bought in excess of 62,000 season tickets. And why not? Most of them believe that the NCAA punishment was unfair and that others are getting away with the same offenses. Perhaps most ironic is the realization that their team is still eligible for the national championship and capable of winning it.

The situations at SMU and TCU were somewhat different than Florida. Playing in the shadow of the Dallas Cowboys, both programs were losing on the field and at the gate during the seventies.

SMU revitalized its football program under Coach Ron Meyer with the illegal assistance of an overly enthusiastic group of boosters. With players being paid for their services, Mustang football came out of the doldrums under Meyer and his successor, Bobby Collins, who recorded a 32–4–1 record during 1982–84. The resurrection commanded a heavy price, however: a three-year probation, the loss of forty-five scholarships over two years, no television in 1986, and no bowls during 1985 and 1986.

TCU came back, albeit briefly, from the bottom of the heap. Having recorded the third worst winning percentage (16.9%) between 1973 and 1983 and averaging just 20,500 fans per game in 1984, the Horned Frogs were 8–4 in their second season under Coach Jim Wacker, including an appearance in the Bluebonnet Bowl. Things were looking even better for 1985 with Heisman candidate Kenneth Davis leading the team. After an opening win over Tulane, two TCU players revealed that they had been receiving regular cash payments from boosters. By week's end they and four others including Davis had been suspended from the team. As a result TCU has reverted to its losing pattern.

In both cases, schools with poor football support systems, fighting a losing battle with the Dallas Cowboys for limited entertainment dollars, had to resort to big-time cheating. By paying good salaries and fringes, they were able to recruit enough talent to win. And as winners they were an attractive show, at least attractive enough to tap a share of the latent Dallas–Fort Worth regional market. Without super talent, however, neither team is likely to succeed in that market.

The penalties seem to have had no effect upon the appeal of the guilty universities to the majority of potential recruits, and they are not stiff enough to dissuade the rule breakers. The new "death penalty" introduced as a result of the 1985 emergency NCAA convention was designed to inhibit future rule breakers. Unfortunately the new penalty, which would suspend competition for one year, is a response to the symptoms and not the cause of the problem. Cheating stems from the irrational pressure to win. Coaches and boosters bend and break the recruiting rules in pursuit of their prey.

Once landed, the student athlete is subjected to inordinate time demands—time demands that frequently preclude progress toward a degree. Until tough restraints are placed on boosters and limits are imposed on the time devoted to sport, there can be no meaningful change.

Only one conclusion can be drawn. Cheating is much more widespread than the number of NCAA sanctions between 1952 and 1985 indicate. The NCAA responds to complaints. It is not an effective monitoring agency like the CIA or FBI. It has a small, though recently increased, enforcement staff. To police the recruitment and the on-campus care of athletes effectively would require a staff of five hundred Columbos and a budget that would paralyze the system.

Why Cheat?

Why do schools cheat? There are several reasons. The commercial atmosphere that hovers over big-time sport is a major contributor. Schools are in the entertainment business—a business separate in almost all respects from their primary educational purpose. They must offer a quality product to their customers to insure success, and that quality product is a good team, year after year.

Revenues are highly correlated with success. Just a few bad years in succession can spell disaster. Therefore, to insure quality a constant flow of outstanding athletes must be brought into the program.

The entire collegiate athletic business has grown larger because many institutions—often spurred by state legislatures—have decreed that football and basketball must be entirely self-supporting. At some schools the big two are even expected to carry the rest of the athletic program. Under these circumstances the pressures to produce have become extraordinarily intense. The best coaches and athletic directors are astute and bright people; they apply sophisticated business management technology to their programs. Constantly pushing for better playing and training facilities, VIP seating, and the frills associated with a consumption-oriented society, they have forced costs upward. Thus they meet any reform movement that could dilute their product with both guns blazing. The fans are another factor in the cheating mess. Loyalty to one's school is commendable. Fanatical attachment to a school's athletic teams, however, can frequently lead to trouble. Alums and friends of the university, eager to support a winner, often go overboard with gifts and favors to athletes and coaches. This preoccupation with winning and the unfortunate tendency to equate it with a university's prestige have been responsible for a great deal of illegal activity. In fact, at many schools the under-the-table giving is well organized, and at some it is coordinated by a full-time solicitor.

Numerous student-athletes now expect something extra, and their attitude is not difficult to comprehend. At many institutions they are truly underpaid. And at the really successful schools, income from football greatly exceeds expenditures on athletic scholarships and fringe benefits. An NCAA football scholarship, measured on an hourly basis, pays recipients less than the minimum wage and has been estimated by some to be as low as sixty cents an hour. Boys from poor circumstances are particularly susceptible to taking a little extra. Roy Danforth, former basketball coach at Tulane, speaks of the unique problems of the athlete: "We take a player out of the ghetto or at least a lower economic level and put him into a college atmosphere. Often the youngster is unable to dress like the other students. It is certainly embarrassing to him— and to me."[8] With more and more boys being plucked from the ghetto and taken to the foreign surroundings of a college campus, it is no wonder that so many are looking under the table for help.

Given the circumstances surrounding athletic recruiting and the personal stake in winning that marks the coaching profession, it is not difficult to appreciate why cheating is so prevalent. The pressure on coaches is intense. Their occupation is chiefly characterized by a retention formula that starts with winning.

Darrell Royal resigned after twenty consecutive winning years at Texas because "the minuses of coaching outweigh the pluses."

The enjoyment was gone. In an interview with Murray Olderman, Royal blasted recruiting. "There's a lot of hypocrisy and outright cheating. The athletic scene must be getting too big. The tail is a whole lot bigger than the dog. Coaches who have won get to feeling all powerful and that the university is in operation just so they can have a football team. Inevitably these people self-destruct."[9]

Frank Broyles, who also resigned after the 1976 season, concluding a highly successful (144–58–1) 19-year tenure at Arkansas, seconds Royal: "The public is expecting perfection out of everybody. I don't believe that over 5 percent of the head coaches today will be head coaches ten years from now [He was close!], because of the demands that people place on them, on recruiting, on everything. People are going to be dropping out voluntarily."[10]

Apparently a little cheating buys time in what at best can be described as an insecure profession. A system that places universities in the professional entertainment business, utilizes quasi-amateur performers, involves all sorts of nonuniversity people, places sole emphasis on winning, and pressures coaches beyond reasonable limits cannot survive indefinitely.

We have already discussed the myriad frustrations of the recruiting game. Uncounted hours are wasted by the boys, the coaches, the faculty advisors, the coed entertainers, and university presidents. Many high school athletes develop an inflated opinion of their own worth. Others are let down hard when they don't receive an offer.

The recruiting game—its national dimensions, high costs, reliance on people from outside the university community, and pervasive dishonesty—is collegiate sport's most miserable affliction. Football and basketball are frequently business operations disguised as extracurricular university activities. At most of the big-name schools, athletic departments are separate entities, often possessing budgetary independence. Unfortunately, the glue that binds them to the university is all too often simply a matter of location: they are in the same place!

Many athletic departments are the antithesis of what the university is supposed to be, a place in which the pursuit of truth and

162

knowledge can be carried on in an environment of honesty and intellectual integrity. To bring a person to an institution for the primary purpose of athletic competition is not in keeping with these purposes, and even less so is the special treatment afforded the athlete on campus, treatment that effectively separates him from the mainstream of university life.

Before 1980 the press emphasized the financial woes that hampered intercollegiate sport, and until then the NCAA cure was heavily focused on monetary difficulties. But nothing improved, because finances were only the symptom of the problem. The most serious issues facing intercollegiate sport were and still are ethical in nature. Should universities actively seek athletes, subsidize them, separate them from the general student body, allow them to enroll in dead-end curricula, ignore or condone grade manipulation, and in general contribute to the preservation of a blatantly hypocritical system? The American university's involvement in athletics must be painstakingly evaluated. Why have we allowed the athletic system to develop as it has, and what viable alternatives are there?

10
What
Can Be
Done?

Are there workable solutions to the problems which currently face big-time intercollegiate sport? Many remedies have been suggested, with critics at one extreme insisting that universities should get out of the sport entertainment business altogether. At the other extreme are those who call for an organization of superpowers, schools that can truly afford the cost of running a major athletic program, which would constitute a semiprofessional league at the college level. Still others have recommended that athletic departments be removed from direct university control.

Between these extremes there are a number of compromise solutions. They include formats for regional athletic recruiting, establishment of grant-in-aid or need programs, abandonment of scholarships for minor sports, and a variety of de-emphasis schemes.

The regional recruiting setups which have thus far been suggested center on the establishment of recruiting territories. The territory within which each institution would recruit would be based on a distance formula. For example, a university at point X could recruit players within a certain mile radius of that point.

Such an area would always include the state in which the university is located and could encompass a number of surrounding states. In some cases, recruiting throughout a state would be allowed even if only a part of that state fell within the circle. Other plans would allow recruiting only in the area within the circle itself.

The circle plan is simple, but it has some serious drawbacks. It assumes that all schools have *equal* access to a supply of potential athletes. As we have seen, this is definitely not the case. Universities in lightly populated Wyoming, Colorado, and Utah would have only a fraction of the choice of those located in New York, Pennsylvania, and Ohio. The universities of Wyoming, Utah, Colorado, and New Mexico, as well as many like them, would soon be out of the big-time athletic business. They would be competing for a severely limited supply of athletes, and none of the schools would obtain enough good players to field a competitive team. It is obvious that if regional recruiting is to be the answer, a more sophisticated system must be developed.

Sports Illustrated's John Underwood has gone a step farther. In a September 1976 piece entitled "Tell You What To Do," he suggests that each institution be assigned to a designated recruiting territory based on "spheres of influence drawn up by areas, to include X number of high schools engaged in tackle football. Take as an arbitrary base 150 schools and 10,000 athletes. If a coach doesn't have that many high school players in his home state, make a circle out from his school until you encompass those numbers. You *can't* physically recruit outside the circle."[1]

He proceeds to argue that such a system would not only cut costs, but also serve to build a local interest by keeping the outstanding local talent at home. The Underwood scheme would require most boys to attend colleges in their home state or home region.

Underwood's plan is an improvement upon the elemental circle method, because it allows for differences in population density. What it fails to take into account are the pronounced regional differences in the quality of the high school game. We have seen that Texas and Ohio high school football is far superior to that played in

Indiana or New York. In fact, these regional differences, combined with the desire of so many institutions to have bigger and better programs, have produced the massive interregional flows of football talent. By prohibiting interregional migration, the Underwood plan would insure success in the high school talent hotbeds — Texas, Mississippi, Ohio, Pennsylvania, California, and Illinois — and sentence schools in Kentucky, the Carolinas, the Big Eight, and the Western Athletic Conference to permanent mediocrity.

If regional recruiting is to be a part of the solution, there is a better way to go about it. There is a more sophisticated geographical solution to the chaotic recruiting that now exists. Regional recruiting, in fundamental terms, represents an attempt to reduce the amount of movement of players across the country. It calls for a halt to the migration of Pennsylvanians to Arizona and Californians to Indiana. It means an end to *national* recruiting.

By utilizing TRANSUB, a computer program which first allocates players to the home state, then minimizes the distance they may travel to out-of-state schools, it is possible to redistribute athletic talent far more efficiently. TRANSUB, which was refined by my fellow geographer Stephen W. Tweedie, is based on two operating principles. The first requires that the major universities in each state recruit players from that state as needed to complete their roster deficiencies. The second requires that any surplus of major college talent be distributed to adjacent states in such a way as to minimize the aggregate travel distance of the total player surplus. The system described here is based on the 1971–72 player production data – where the talent came from — and the location, by state, of all universities with big-time football and basketball programs. With minor adjustments it is applicable to the current situation.

The changes in the geography of football recruiting under this system would be dramatic (figures 58 and 59). The amount of interstate movement would be cut by approximately 80 percent!

Pennsylvania, which actually sent ten or more football players to seventeen different states, is an excellent case in point. Under

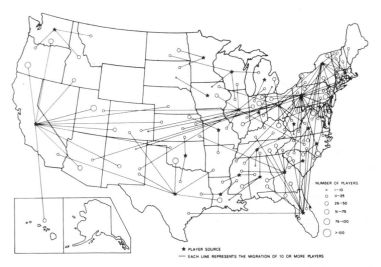

Figure 58. Actual migratory behavior of college-bound football players (major colleges, as designated by the NCAA and NAIA and including a 100 percent sample from each state) (data base: 1971–72, 1976–77, 1980–81 rosters).

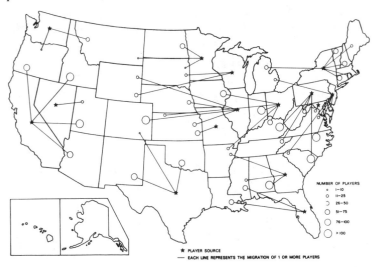

Figure 59. Optimizing migratory behavior of college-bound football players (major colleges, as designated by the NCAA and NAIA and including a 100 percent sample from each state) (data base: 1971–72, 1976–77 rosters).

the regional recruiting system the state of Pennsylvania would supply all of the players that its major universities—Penn State, Pittsburgh, Temple, and Pennsylvania—demanded, and then ship large numbers to South Carolina, West Virginia, Tennessee, and Kentucky. This could be facilitated by establishing a December signing date of in-state recruits and a February date for those wishing to play elsewhere.

The New York surplus would be allocated in similar fashion. After local demands—Syracuse, Cornell, and Colgate—had been met, the remaining athletes would move out to Michigan, Vermont, New Hampshire, Maine, Massachusetts, and Rhode Island. The Illinois footballers would go west to Kansas, Colorado, Nebraska, and Wyoming. Only California would operate in essentially the same way as it does now, with its surplus going to Oregon, Idaho, Utah, and Arizona.

Basketball is not as complicated as football because there are only about one-third as many players involved (figures 60 and 61). The optimization procedure would change the directional flow of the recruits. Illinois would supply states to the West; Indiana and Ohio, to the South and Southwest; and New York to the East. California would continue to export to the Far West. Interstate flows in the South and in the Atlantic Coast Conference region would be halted. Southeastern Conference and Atlantic Coast Conference schools would utilize their own talent first and then import from the Midwest and New Jersey. The Washington, D.C., surplus could be directed south instead of north.

What would be the benefits and drawbacks to such a recruiting plan for collegiate football and basketball? It must be remembered that this regional recruiting format is based on reality. These data include the locations of all universities attempting to field big-time football and basketball teams and the locations of all high school athletes who were recruited to the major institutions during the 1968–72 time period. Perhaps the most obvious benefit is that the competition for the best high school players would be substantially curtailed, and therefore the costs of obtaining these players would also be cut. Competition would essentially be among the institu-

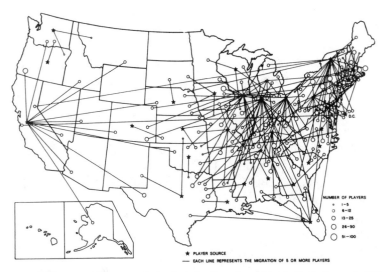

Figure 60. Actual migratory behavior of college-bound basketball players (a 100 percent sample of major colleges and a 50 percent sample of minor colleges from each state) (data base: 1971–72, 1976–77 rosters).

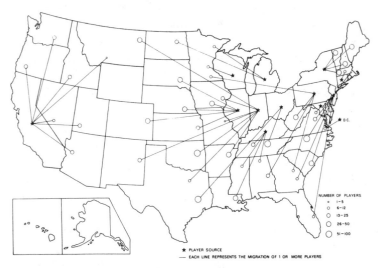

Figure 61. Optimizing migratory behavior of college-bound basketball players (a 100 percent sample of major colleges and a 50 percent sample of minor colleges from each state) (data base: 1971–72, 1976–77 rosters).

tions in each state for the high school boys in that state. For those states with a shortage of high school talent, the competition would go beyond the state boundaries and include the other states designated as their suppliers. If such a plan were adopted, the distance traveled by each athlete and recruiter would be substantially reduced. Therefore, the cost of recruiting the athletes—and the temptations to cheat on the far off blue-chip market—would also decrease.

There are drawbacks to any type of regional recruiting. The athletes would suffer most. They could no longer offer their services to the highest bidder, and their freedom of choice would be severely restricted.

Presently, any person with collegiate athletic potential can select virtually any school in the nation. This freedom—in addition to the mounting demand for winning teams—has spawned the financial and ethical problems that now exist. Under the proposed regional recruiting plan, an athlete would be limited to his home state or to a group of nearby states. There would also be an unequal degree of freedom of choice with respect to the number and quality of university programs available to the athlete. Athletes living in deficit states like Indiana or Alabama would have fewer choices than those residing in surplus states such as Illinois, Pennsylvania, or Texas. For example, a California boy could select from universities in five to seven states, while a South Carolinian would have to choose between staying home to play at South Carolina, Clemson, the Citadel or Furman, or going to Georgia or Georgia Tech. Californians could select from among ten Division IA schools at home or ten in surrounding states.

The outcry from the big-time powers would be audible in Siberia if such changes were implemented. "We will recruit anywhere we please!" Undoubtedly this type of impingement would encounter strong opposition in a society as free as ours. Some type of compromise plan could be developed so as to allow a certain amount of migration and at the same time restrict the total freedom that now exists. One possibility would be the establishment of a percentage formula. This would permit schools in a given state to

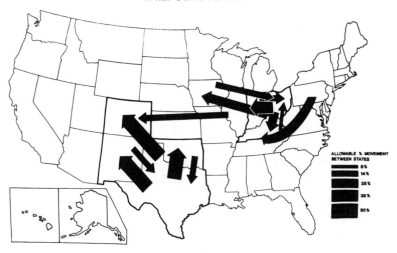

Figure 62. Sample recruiting districts.

recruit somewhere between 10 and 30 percent of their athletes from outside the designated recruiting territory. The percentage could be set on the basis of current and past recruiting behavior. States that have come to rely on foreign products could still do so, but to a lesser extent than at present. Those recruiting primarily at home would not be affected much by any rule change.

Another plausible variation of the regional recruiting optimization plan would involve the creation of recruiting districts (figure 62). Boundaries could be drawn so as to group a surplus state with one or more deficit states. Percentages of in-state and out-of-state recruits could then be set up for each state in the district. For example, surplus states like California or Pennsylvania might be required to procure 80 percent of their athletes locally whereas deficit states like Utah and Indiana might be assigned values ranging from 50 to 80 percent.

By applying this formula to a few combinations of states we can see the basic form of the recruiting district. One variation would group Ohio, a surplus state, with Indiana, a deficit state. Ohio schools would be limited to a 20 percent Indiana quota—six of thirty scholarships—while Indiana schools could recruit up to 50 percent of their players from Ohio.

Under this arrangement Ohio players would have a slightly greater range of choice than they would have had in the original version of the regional recruiting model. The Ohio district could be expanded to include Kentucky and Iowa. Based on the optimization formula, Kentucky would be allowed to obtain 20 percent of its players from Ohio, and Iowa could obtain 35 percent. In return, Ohio would be given an 8 percent Kentucky allotment and a 14 percent credit in Iowa. There would be no reciprocal privileges among Indiana, Kentucky, and Iowa.

Moving to the Southwest, the Texas surplus would be grouped with Oklahoma, New Mexico, and Colorado to constitute a four-state recruiting district. Oklahoma and New Mexico would be allowed to bring in 40 percent of their players from Texas, but Colorado would be limited to just a few players per year. On the other hand, Texas institutions if they so desired could recruit up to 16 percent of their needs from Oklahoma and New Mexico.

The establishment of recruiting districts on the basis of the computerized allocation procedure would require some states—Colorado, Kansas, and Kentucky, for example—to belong to more than one recruiting district. Colorado would be seeking talent in both Texas and Illinois, while Kentucky would search in Ohio and Pennsylvania. Much of the multiplicity could be removed, though, by setting contiguity restraints on the allocations.

Another solution to the recruiting problem takes into account the state-to-state migrations of all undergraduate students in the United States. Approximately 17 percent of the undergraduate students in this country attend a university outside of their home state. This is a small fraction when compared to the interstate athletic movement. Fifty-seven percent of the football players and 53 percent of the basketball players, as measured by the 1971–72 rosters, crossed state lines to attend college.

It would be a rather routine procedure to analyze the geographical sources of each major university's undergraduate student population. Athletic recruitment would then be programmed to draw from the same areas and in the same proportions as the undergraduate student body. Flexibility could be added by merging this plan with the regional recruitment plan.

Let's face it—regional recruiting is not apt to occur soon. There are many legal questions to be answered and attitudes to be changed before any type of regional system could be implemented. The prospects for regional solutions are dim in light of the fanatical opposition to recent NCAA limitations on the number of scholarships, coaches, and players on traveling squads.

The NCAA members have voted most of their reforms on the basis of financial duress, electing to ignore the deeper ethical and moral problems that are tearing at the soul of intercollegiate sport. The move to separate the really big-time, or "super," football schools from the hordes of smaller schools that comprise the great majority of the NCAA membership finally succeeded in 1978 with the establishment of Division IA. Barry Switzer put it quite succinctly in 1976:

We ought to institute a new conference immediately. Made up of all those universities who demonstrate a serious commitment to football. Provide a substantial number of full scholarships for the income sports of football and basketball. Eighty more scholarships for the minor sports to be allocated as each university preferred. We just want to associate ourselves with other schools like us who have a commitment to excellence.[2]

An Amateur Alternative

It doesn't have to go that far. There is still time to get collegiate sport back into perspective. The Ivy League, that hollowed cradle of collegiate sport, saw the light long ago. In explaining and justifying the 1951 decision to de-emphasize athletics, presidents James B. Conant of Harvard, Whitney Griswold of Yale, and Harold Dodds of Princeton stated:

A student takes part in college athletics because of the value of the experience for him, and he has the same obligation as other students, to assume responsibility for solving his educational problems. Any other view seems to us a distortion of educational and moral values.[3]

Stressing the importance of athletics in a sound college educational program, the statement asserted, nevertheless, that all aspects of college athletics were subordinate to the essential purposes for which colleges existed:

> The athletic program exists for the welfare of the student, for the contribution it can make to his healthy educational experience, not for the glorification of the individual or the prestige or profit of the college. The academic work and the physical work of the student are primary.
>
> No individual should be exploited for the sake of athletic success. No athletic scholarships or special subsidies of any sort for athletes are given by Harvard, Yale or Princeton.[4]

Despite a contrary view from the West, today's Ivy League teams play a respectable brand of football and basketball. They do so without benefit of athletic scholarships, off-season practices, or the cajoling, coddling, and payment of student athletes.

The Ivy League gave collegiate football some of its most memorable moments. Walter Camp's innovative genius helped to spawn what we now call the collegiate game. George Plimpton eloquently places the Ivy League decision in perspective:

> The storied rivalries that started during the 1870s; . . . the towering names (Heffelfinger, Kelley and Booth of Yale, Brickley and Mahan of Harvard, Warner of Cornell, Poe of Princeton, Oberlander of Dartmouth, Luckman and Montgomery of Columbia . . .); the eyepopping legends (Coach Percy Haughton was supposed to have throttled a bull dog to death to pep up his Harvard team before the 1908 Yale game); the huge, frenzied crowds of the '20s; the great marching songs; those literary heroes Dink Stover and Frank Merriwell of Yale; a whole flapper generation that identified with Eastern football; the coonskin coat and the flask and all the attendant rituals and ceremonials of those New England autumn afternoons. Now all of this brilliant history and panoply was being shunted toward an obscure and shameful end, with the quality of the football withering to such a degree that surely the teams, in the vast empty places of their past glory, would play surreal contests as informal and ignored as pickup games in the corner of a municipal park.

But now, because nothing like that happened, many observers believe that the Ivy League's adoption of a more balanced concept of football may be as important to the progress of the game, and perhaps to its future elsewhere, as what the colleges provided at its genesis.[5]

The Ivy League started it, overemphasized it to the point that the Carnegie Foundation report was assembled, and finally came to the realization that the goals of higher education and big-time football were incompatible. League rivalries, however, are still as intense as any in the country.

If faculties and students were to stand up and demand that big-time collegiate sport be cleansed, the Ivy League system could serve as a model for intercollegiate sports. Enforcement of the amateur code would have to be worlds better than it is now, and penalties for those who violate the code would have to be even more severe than those passed by the NCAA in 1985. Until coaches, players, and university administrators are severely punished, the cheating is bound to persist. Pros wouldn't like it, but no one can deny that everyone—students, faculty, alumni, and, most important, student-athletes—would be far better off than they are now.

A purely amateur system would represent a purification, a cleansing, and a return to past values. Though a long shot, at least for the entertainment-oriented programs, I am compelled to suggest some basic ground rules. Even if they are unacceptable at the Division IA institutions they could be applied throughout the remainder of the schools offering collegiate sports.

I recommend the following guidelines for implementing a system of amateur collegiate sports:
1. No freshmen eligibility for intercollegiate sports
2. A maximum of ten hours of on-field practice per week
3. A maximum of two hours of film review and team meetings per week
4. No more than five hours of required weight training per week
5. No Sunday film sessions or meetings

6. No recruiting
7. No spring practice for football or off-season practice for other sports
8. No preschool practice, combined with a mid-September starting date for football and a spring semester or winter quarter starting date for basketball
9. A scheduling arrangement for all sports that would allow a maximum of seven days of missed classes
10. A severe penalty system that would punish coaches, players, and institutions guilty of violating the rules
11. Elimination of alumni and other outsiders from any direct involvement with university athletic affairs (the temptation to be involved under these circumstances would probably be minimal).

Under such a system the quality of intercollegiate sport performance would go down. But our entertainment-oriented universities would still field excellent teams. They have a tradition and access to very talented student-athletes. The best athletes would probably still attend the big-name schools, at least to the extent that they do under the present framework. There would still be bowl games and postseason tournaments. And a hierarchy of competition would still exist.

The maintenance of the amateur code would require the cooperation of all institutions. Cheating in any form could not be tolerated. Violators of the code, coaches and athletes, would be banned from further involvement.

The amateur alternative for our universities might generate the establishment of minor-professional leagues for those athletes not interested in a college education. Baseball has traditionally developed its talent in the minor leagues, though colleges have recently increased their baseball-training component. Football and basketball need a minor league option for college-age talent. Fifty teams, perhaps featuring job training, would meet the needs of the nonstudent-athletes.

Perhaps a rebirth of amateurism makes too much sense. It may be too utopian—students competing in sports on the side rather than athletes taking courses on the side. Universities have gotten off track. Sports for sport's sake has given way to sports for profit and fame. It's time to seriously reconsider the Ivy League decision in 1951 to put collegiate sport back into perspective. Athletic programs should indeed exist for the welfare of the student.

I would like to see it happen, but it probably can't, at least for now, because there is too much invested in athletic programs in other sections of the United States. This is particularly true among the major conferences throughout the South, the Midwest, and the Great Plains. There, college football is a major form of public entertainment. Professional football is widely dispersed, not available to most Americans. High-quality live entertainment is hard to find in many areas, and collegiate sport fills the void. Entire states and special segments of the population have come to identify with *their* team. Support is stronger and expectations are higher than they would be in the Ivy League model, and they will not wither away overnight, regardless of how out of proportion the whole business has become.

Given the grim reality of the situation—the commercialism and hypocrisy—a more plausible solution is in order. Let's admit that colleges are in the entertainment business and that university and state pride are worth paying for. Once this is acknowledged, we can seek honest answers and begin to cope with the moral decay that pervades big-time collegiate sport.

11
The
Practical
Solution

There is a practical solution to the ethical and economic problems which plague big-time athletics: separate the athletic function, the revenue sports, from the traditional form of university control and allow a select group of collegiate football and basketball teams to become second-order, or minor league if you prefer, professional franchises located in the university communities.[1] The teams would utilize university facilities such as stadiums, arenas, athletic dormitories, practice fields, and weight rooms; and in place of the present student-athlete arrangement, players would be given the option of attending the university, without interruption, during the off-season. Spring football practice would be replaced by a late summer training camp and possibly a two- or three-game exhibition season. Basketball would be confined to the spring semester and the holiday break that immediately precedes it.

By professionalizing big-time football and basketball and methods of player acquisition, both the distasteful aspects of recruiting and the unethical practices so often associated with maintaining athletes on campus would be eliminated. The on-campus hypocrisy would no longer be necessary. There would be no need for watered-down courses, brain coaches, special tutors, educational motivation directions, transcript meddling, and jock-favoring professors and alumni. Universities would be sponsoring openly professional programs and players would be sharing in the revenues they produce.

A major flaw in the present "amateur" system is the huge gap between player-generated revenues and the payments that the players receive for their services. This is particularly true in the case of big-time football. The most successful programs are now producing revenues in excess of $10 million annually, although their player costs average less than $1 million. The "profits" are utilized to generously reimburse athletic administrators, coaches, and their support personnel and to underwrite the so-called non-revenue sports. Football players provide a substantial slice of the funds necessary to subsidize golfers, tennis players, swimmers, gymnasts, and other athletes in whom the student body and the public has little interest.

Thus numerous football and basketball players are failing to share in the revenues they generate. Furthermore they are risking injuries that often jeopardize their future earning capacity. Instead of being paid their fair share for work completed, they are compensated in the form of room, board, tuition, and books. For many who are unable to obtain a college education or not interested in one the compensation represents no more than room and board. It is no wonder that so many have demanded and received additional payments for their services. And from the perspective of economic justice they are fully deserving of payment for services rendered.

A recent comment by Dale Brown, LSU basketball coach echoes this view:

> We've got to change the system. Pay the athletes a few hundred dollars a month for their basic needs. You're going to hear the reverse— "My kid goes to LSU and has to work at McDonald's [to earn money]." But your kid doesn't make $2 million [the rough yearly gross income from basketball] for LSU. Who's making the money from sports? The

athletic director, coaches, doctors, trainers, airlines, hotels—we don't mention the whorehouses and massage parlors. The athletes are treated like migrant workers.

The NCAA doesn't solve the problem; they keep putting talcum powder on a cancer. They legislate against human dignity. I'll tell you what you're going to have left in this [coaching] profession. A bunch of narcissistic, money-hungry sonofabitches that love to see themselves on TV in their three-piece suits and alligator shoes, because good people are fed up with the crap you've got to go through. I just want to be left alone. I have to be up in Aspen with a bottle of wine.[2]

Brown and others believe that the present system is destined for self-destruction. If players were allowed to share in the fruits of their labor, big-time sport would be an honest business operation designed to entertain the university community, alumni, and other interested parties. Those players who wanted a college education could get one, and those who didn't would be free to pursue whatever off-season jobs they wished.

Under a professional scheme the number of players on the football team could be reduced from the existing NCAA limit of ninety-five, plus "walk-ons," to somewhere between fifty and sixty. A minimum-maximum salary schedule would have to be negotiated for the entire system. Each player would receive a starting salary representative of his real worth, and the cost would not be significantly greater than that of present scholarship subsidies. Basketball salaries could also be scaled according to projected income. Teams could get by with five coaches instead of eight or ten. If the system could be explained and presented as an honest, forthright replacement of what now exists, student and alumni support would remain strong and might even grow.

It is entirely possible that our national fixation with intercollegiate football is rooted in the myth that most big-time athletes are truly students representing their alma mater in the noble pursuit of glory. It is possible that we are supporting an irrational intercollegiate athletic system because we are comfortable with the myth and symbolism that encompass it. Discussions with my students and a wide range of collegiate sports enthusiasts strongly suggest that a professional-collegiate system is workable. Affiliation with university communities will assure the maintenance of the hallowed football weekend and all that it entails. There would still be student bands, cheerleaders, pompom girls, homecoming, parents' days and all the other elements that make the American intercollegiate athletic scene such a unique and exhilarating phenomenon.

The separation of big-time athletic programs from the universities would not eliminate traditional forms of intercollegiate competition. Teams of full-time, nonsubsidized students in a variety of sports could be funded from the educational budget. Sports could revert to their original status of relatively low pressure extracurricular activities. In so doing they would once again serve the function for which they were originated—the provision of vigorous physical activity and recreation for the *student* body.

Justification for a Super League

How would a super league of collegiate football be organized? Who would the members be? Before answering those questions, a review of certain events that have produced the current geographical organization of both professional and collegiate football is in order. We begin with the premise that the hysteria surrounding football at Nebraska, Texas, Notre Dame, Oklahoma, Alabama, Michigan, Ohio State, and other places is an outgrowth of a real and sometimes desperate need, an expression of an atavistic pride of school and the place it represents. High-quality live entertainment is wanted everywhere, not just in the big cities where the professional franchises are located, and so the colleges have moved in to fill the entertainment voice.

Most of the collegiate powers have evolved in smaller cities located in sparsely populated TV market areas. This remoteness of location has often contributed to the profound need of local inhabitants for some sort of recognition—a place in the limelight. Thus success in intercollegiate sports has become a means of attracting national attention to *their* place and their university. Today, teams like Oklahoma, Nebraska, LSU, Ohio State, and Wyoming are viewed by loyal supporters as representatives of their respective states, and their influence extends far beyond campus and community boundaries.

The present geographical arrangement of professional and big-time college football teams is in many ways a product of decisions made in professional baseball during the nineteenth century. Major league baseball franchises were locationally stable during the first half of this century, a period that witnessed the rapid development of both collegiate and professional football. The collegiate game developed first, sinking roots in many of the places where it thrives today. After a token small-town beginning, professional football (the forerunner of the NFL was established in 1920) gradually moved into the same cities and market areas that harbored professional baseball. As a result, the colleges continued to provide an increasingly more sophisticated form of sports entertainment to those not living in the major northeastern and midwestern cities.

Major league baseball owners had set the tone. They vigorously opposed any alterations to the locational pattern of their sport. Not a single team changed cities between 1901 and 1953, nor were there any expansion clubs. In 1960 there were still only sixteen major league teams, the same number that had served 76 million Americans in 1900.

The baseball brass allowed no expansion or franchise movements during the fifty-year period that witnessed a doubling of the population of the United States. Some have said the problem was transportation, but reliance on surface transportation certainly did not prohibit the establishment of teams in Milwaukee, Baltimore, Montreal, Toronto, Louisville, Newark, Jersey City, Columbus, or Kansas City. Facilities were not the problem either. During the fifties, when franchise relocation became popular, several teams moved to cities in advance of stadium construction. No, the problem was simply an establishment that was dominated by selfish motives and an overwhelming inertia.

Apparently the baseball establishment believed that the minor leagues could satisfy the American appetite for live baseball. The first half of the present century was marked by the ubiquitous diffusion of minor league teams. It was rare for a place with 25,000 or more inhabitants to be without a minor league club. At the peak, prior to major league relocation and expansion, there were fifty-nine minor leagues and over 500 teams. Televised broadcasts of major league games took an immediate toll on the minors, effectively reordering the geographical structure of the system. By 1951 there was a drop to 360 teams and 49 leagues, and as of the 1985 season there were just 120 teams and 15 leagues. Small-town residents no longer have their own team; their loyalties have shifted to the majors and to other leisure pursuits.

When major league sports expansion finally did come, it brought in the ''new'' metropolises of the South and the West. The process was hastened by the infusion of nonestablishment capital, savvy, and enthusiasm. This infusion was responsible for the creation of the American Football League, the American Basketball Association, and the World Hockey League. The advent of jet transportation also helped, but the key to professional expansion was the presence of massive pent-up demand. A great segment of urban America had no access to big-time sport. When professional baseball, football, basketball, and other sports were finally established in previously unserved markets, support for them was almost universal.

As interest increased, media coverage also grew. This in turn produced more discussion and conversation about sporting events. The gathering momentum, particularly with respect to football, combined with technical breakthroughs in television broadcasting, prompted an explosion of sport specials and sports-related gimmickry.

Thus American society, in possession of more leisure time and more money, has become increasingly engrossed with sport. Professional football has been the growth leader in terms of the number of new followers since 1950. The public interest spawned by professional football—with its preoccupation with specialization and the perfection of technique—has also infected the universities. Funds invested in coaches, recruiting, athletic scholarships, and living quarters have grown so rapidly that many schools, in trying to keep pace, have experienced severe financial stress. The colleges are imitating the pros in the drive for perfection. In the process, many have lost sight of the recreational and extracurricular purposes that intercollegiate sports were designed to serve.

In summary, it appears that the expansion of teams and public interest during the past thirty years simply represents the satisfaction of a tremendous backlog of demand. The availability of live sports entertainment had failed to keep pace with population growth. A cautionary note is appropriate here, however, for like many other good things the expansion of professional football was carried to an extreme. The most recent efforts, the World Football League, and the USFL were busts. There were too many locational mistakes, and as a result the fledgling World Football League teams couldn't attract enough support to compete with either the NFL or the universities.

The NFL does attempt to avoid direct competition with collegiate football. True, the pros have inflicted irreparable damage upon the collegiate game in some places—Miami, Philadelphia, New York City, Dallas, Fort Worth, and Atlanta. But for the foreseeable future, professional expansion will probably be insignificant, and if new teams are added, they will not be placed near the strongholds of collegiate football.

Understanding of the pattern of development of the geography of American football requires a comprehension of collegiate-professional location characteristics (figure 63). It must be kept in mind that the big-time collegiate programs got under way much earlier than the professional teams. The most important period for the development of collegiate football was between 1890 and 1930. The glory days of professional football came much later.

The location of most of the big-time colleges is a function of U.S. political divisions. Historically, the states have placed a premium on establishing and nurturing their universities. Most states have at least one major public institution and many, including New

Figure 63. Location of NFL franchises and major college football programs, 1985.

York, Ohio, Illinois, Texas, and California, have groups of schools situated to serve their various regional markets. Virtually all of the states—regardless of population or location—have elected to support big-time football programs at at least one of their institutions. Added to these are a number of randomly located private universities also engaging in big-time football.

Most of the colleges have opted to join some type of athletic conference (chapter 7). The conferences typically promote competition among universities located in the same region. In general, those leagues whose location was, or still is, remote from the concentration of pro teams have developed the most costly and most successful programs. The Big Eight, Southwest, Pacific Ten and Southeastern conferences generally conform to this rule. A tendency to place greater emphasis on football in those areas has served to elevate the status of the college game. In some of these places the collegiate game has actually taken the place of professional football as an entertainment medium. It would seem that the extreme demand for excellence that characterizes the strongholds of intercollegiate football is a result of the geographically limited availability of professional opportunities. Conversely, if professional football were more widespread, the pressures for excellence at the intercollegiate level would probably abate. But as it now stands, supporters and benefactors demand excellence regardless of whether the teams are composed of pros or collegians.

Returning to the initial questions, who and where should the superpowers be? For many years, the classification of major football and basketball teams was left to the sportswriters. They decided *who* was a major power. Finally, in 1964, the NCAA began to develop its own criteria. It inaugurated Division II football playoffs, thereby relegating certain schools to secondary status. Then in 1968, the NCAA developed a TV plan which guaranteed certain conferences and independents a minimum number of appearances, in effect granting superior status to a favored few.

In 1971 the NCAA established a reorganization committee chaired by Ed Sherman of Muskegon College. The committee's work resulted in the establishment of three NCAA divisions by 1973, with the major football powers assigned to Division I. Initially, there were 120 so designated; by 1976 the number had climbed to 136 because of what Tom Hansen, assistant executive director of the NCAA, calls a domino effect.[3] As more and more teams elected to go big time, a reclassification committee was formed and charged with a review of Division I growth. The committee came to the 1976 convention with a recommendation to reduce drastically the number of Division I members. But the recommendation did not provide for an appeal process and the convention voted to table it. In 1976 the reclassification committee, equipped with an appeal process, again recommended a cut in Division I membership, from 136 to a more manageable and realistic 97; but virtually all the schools earmarked for elimination appealed and won.

In 1978, the NCAA membership voted to form a super league — Division IA. At last there would be a reduction of big-time programs. The initial response, however, was a stampede to the top. But finally, after considerable shuffling for position, Division IA football membership has stabilized at 105 schools.

Though it was difficult for the NCAA to control its division lines, the astute football fan knew all along that Rice, Wichita, and Utah State were not in the same class with Michigan, Alabama, and UCLA. There are probably no more than sixty bona fide major college teams. The formation of the College Football Association, whose membership comprises five major conferences and a few independents, lends credence to this assertion (the Big Ten and Pacific Ten have thus far refused to join). Presently the CFA is a public relations and television marketing consortium, but there is a good chance that it may be the first step in a formal break with the NCAA.

It appears, then, that there is a real possibility for radical change in the structure of collegiate football. The time may well be ripe for the proposal put forth at the beginning of this chapter—the formation of a super league of professional teams sponsored by, but not integrally a part of, universities and colleges throughout the country. If such a league is to be organized, the first matter to be decided has to do with where the teams should be located.

THE COMPUTER MODEL

Several approaches can be used to determine the locations where the super league college teams would receive optimum support. To arrive at these optimum sites, we must first consider their locations relative to the present locations of NFL franchises. We must also consider the degree of success which the present major colleges have attained, and we must take into account the profound regional differences in enthusiasm for the sport and in the ability to play the game. The selection of the super league college teams begins with a computer simulation that attempts to optimally locate the NFL and super league college franchises.

Utilizing a location/allocation computer program called LAP, it is possible to simulate an expansion of professional football franchises, based on the actual distribution of the U.S. population. To keep things uncomplicated, we will focus on an expansion program involving a total of 100 teams. We will assume that the 28 existing NFL teams will remain in their current cities, and at this initial stage, we will also assume similar interest levels in football throughout all sections of the country. Our task then is to recommend the best locations for 72 (100 minus the 28 professional teams) superpowers. In theory we are attempting to provide every American with approximately equal access to professional football entertainment, either through the NFL or through the super league college teams. Admittedly a theoretical exercise, it nevertheless constitutes a starting point from whence to evaluate the desirability of both actual and potential locations of NFL and super league college teams.

Prior to beginning the computer analysis, the New York City, Chicago, and Los Angeles metropolitan areas were eliminated from contention. Based on their substantial population (over 13 percent of the national total), six teams are assigned to the New York City metropolitan area, and three each to Chicago and Los Angeles.

After removing these three metropolitan regions from consideration, the United States was divided into eleven areas of equal population. Successive computer runs first identified the best two locations in each area, then four, and finally eight. This procedure resulted in eighty-eight optimal locations, plus those twelve already allocated to the giant urban centers (figure 64).

The computer allocations show where the teams would be if population distribution were the only criterion used in placing them. For example, according to the model, Alabama should have two teams, one in Birmingham and one in Mobile; the single Arkansas team would be in Little Rock; and Ohio would have six (figure 64). Several states have no team at all. As the figure shows, the computer program allows the selection of precise locations. Because some of these locations would not be feasible—having neither a university nor an ample stadium facility—we will, from here on, concentrate on serving the needs of the states. We will

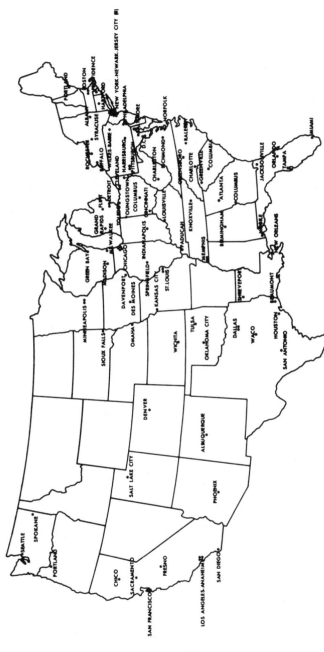

Figure 64. A theoretical market-oriented expansion of professional sports franchises. Franchise locations are based on television market areas. Each franchise serves one or more television market areas.

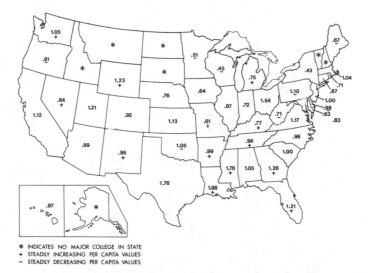

* INDICATES NO MAJOR COLLEGE IN STATE
+ STEADILY INCREASING PER CAPITA VALUES
− STEADILY DECREASING PER CAPITA VALUES

Figure 65. Per capita origin of major college football players (based on place of high school graduation) (data base: 1961–65, 1971, 1977, 1980 rosters).

allow the locations of existing universities and facilities to determine the locations of the super league collegiate teams.

INTEREST-ABILITY INDEX

The next step in the allocation procedure is to rate the states on the basis of football interest and ability. This can be accomplished by utilizing the state player-productivity data introduced in chapter 5. For this calculation, however, the data base has been expanded to encompass major college recruiting between the academic years 1959–60 and 1980–81 (excluding 1967–70), a total of over 55,000 players.

By converting the player origin statistics to per capita form, the relative producing capacities of each state can be assessed (figure 65). To simplify the state-to-state comparisons I have assigned a value of 1.00 to the national average of player production and will hereafter refer to this measure as the *interest-ability index*. Thus a state with an interest-ability index of 1.50 would be breeding 50 percent more players than average. A value of .50 would indicate player output of just one-half the national norm.

The per capita figures, supplemented by the trend symbols, provide an excellent measure of the importance of schoolboy football within each state. For example, Texas has an interest-ability index of 1.78; Mississippi, 1.78; and Ohio, 1.54. The quality of high school football is superior in each state. Relatively large investments have been made in facilities and coaches, and many of the three states' communities are extremely dedicated to the production of highly skilled gridiron specialists. The fever pitch of excitement that surrounds the high school game in those states is matched at their universities.

In marked contrast to Texas, Mississippi, and Ohio are New York, .43; Missouri, .61; and Wisconsin, .45. High school football in the latter three states is of relatively poor quality. Characterized by mediocre facilities, small coaching staffs, and low-key attitudes, it often plays second fiddle to basketball, hockey, soccer, or lacrosse. The high school situation in the three states has been reflected at the collegiate level. Missouri and Wisconsin each have just one major football institution. New York has but four, having chosen to keep big-time football out of its state university system.

There is a significant relationship between the quality of high school football and interest in the collegiate game. It therefore seems reasonable to adjust, for each state, the recommended number of super league collegiate teams on the basis of the interest-ability index. In table 13, which shows the results of these adjustments, note, for example, that the initial computer allocation assigns seven teams to New York, six to Texas, and two to South Carolina. When we subtract the three existing professional franchises in New York and the two in Texas from the recommended allocations, we are left with four new super league collegiate teams assigned to New York, four to Texas, and two to South Carolina (which has no professional franchise). The interest-ability indices are .43 for New York, 1.78 for Texas, and 1.00 for South Carolina. To figure the adjusted recommendation, we multiply the num-

Table 13: Selection of the Super League Franchises

State	Ability Index Norm = 1.00 1961–77 Per Capita Production of Major College Players	No. of Recommended Franchises	Existing NFL Franchises	Projected University Franchises	Projected University Franchises Using Ability Multiplier (Rounded Off)	Attendance	Tradition	Special Situations	Selections
Alabama	1.05	2	0	2	2	2	2		Alabama Auburn
Arkansas	.99	1	0	1	1	1	1		Arkansas
Alaska	0.00	0	0	0	0	0	0		
Arizona	.89	2	0	2	2	2	2		Arizona, Arizona State
California	1.12	8	4	4	4	5	5		California, USC, UCLA, Stanford, San Diego State,[1] San Jose State[1]
Colorado	.92	1	1	0	1	2	2		Colorado, Air Force
Connecticut	.87	1	0	1	1	1	1	0	
Delaware	.98	0	0	0	0	0	0	0	
Dist. of Columbia	.83	2	1	1	1	0	0		
Florida	1.21	5	2	3	3	3	3		Florida, Florida State, Miami

Georgia	1.26	2	1	1	1	2	2		Georgia, Georgia Tech
Hawaii[1]	.97	0	0	0	0	1	0		Hawaii
Idaho	0.00	0	0	0	0	0	0		
Illinois	.87	5	1	4	4	1	2		Illinois
Indiana	.72	2	0	2	1	3	3		Notre Dame, Purdue, Indiana[1]
Iowa	.64	2	0	2	1	2	2		Iowa, Iowa State
Kansas	1.13	1	0	1	1	1	1		Kansas
Kentucky	.77	2	0	2	2	1	1		Kentucky, Louisville[1]
Louisiana	1.98	2	1	1	3	2	3		LSU, Tulane[1]
Maine	.67	1	0	1	1	0	0		
Maryland	.63	2	0	2	1	2	2		Maryland, Navy
Massachusetts	.87	2	1	1	1	1	2	0	Boston College
Michigan	.75	4	1	3	2	2	2		Michigan, Michigan State
Minnesota	.51	2	1	1	1	1	1		Minnesota
Mississippi	1.78	1	0	1	2	2	2		Mississippi, Mississippi State
Missouri	.61	3	2	1	1	1	1		Missouri
Montana	0.00	0	0	0	0	0	0		
Nebraska	.76	1	0	1	1	1	1		Nebraska
Nevada	.84	0	0	0	0	0	0		Nevada,[1] Las Vegas
New Hampshire	0.00	0	0	0	0	0	1		

Table 13: Selection of the Super League Franchises (*continued*)

State	Ability Index Norm=1.00 1961–77 Per Capita Production of Major College Players	No. of Recommended Franchises	Existing NFL Franchises	Projected University Franchises	Projected University Franchises Using Ability Multiplier (Rounded Off)	Attendance	Tradition	Special Situations	Selections
New Mexico	.95	1	0	1	1	0	0	*	
New Jersey	1.00	2	.5*	1	1	1	0	+1	Rutgers
New York	.43	7	2.5*	4	2	2	2		Syracuse, Army
North Carolina	.98	3	0	3	3	3	3		North Carolina, North Carolina State, Duke[2]
North Dakota	0.00	0	0	0	0	0	0		
Ohio	1.54	6	2	4	6	1	3	*	Ohio State, Miami[1] Cincinnati[1]
Oklahoma	1.05	2	0	2	2	2	3		Oklahoma, Oklahoma State, Tulsa[1]
Oregon	.81	1	0	1	1	0	2	*	Oregon or Oregon State[1]
Pennsylvania	1.10	6	2	4	5	2	2		Penn State, Pittsburgh
Rhode Island	.71	1	0	1	1	0	0		

South Carolina	1.00	2	0	2	2	2	2		South Carolina, Clemson
South Dakota	0.00	1	0	1	1	0	0	*	
Texas	1.78	6	2	4	8	4	7		Texas, Texas A&M. Texas Tech. Baylor. Houston. SMU
Tennessee	.96	2	0	2	2	2	1		Tennessee, Memphis State[1]
Utah	1.21	1	0	1	1	1	2		Brigham Young Utah[1]
Vermont	0.00	0	0	0	0	0	0		Vermont
Virginia	1.17	2	0	2	2	2	0		Virginia Tech, Virginia
Washington	1.05	2	1	1	1	1	1		Washington, Washington State
West Virginia	.71	1	0	1	1	1	1		West Virginia
Wisconsin	.45	3	1	2	1	1	1		Wisconsin
Wyoming	1.23	0	0	0	0	0	1	+ 1	Wyoming[1]
OPTIMAL TOTALS	1.00	100	28	73	83	64	74	+ 2	

The non-numbered schools represent the Prime Candidates (see Table 18).
[1] See Table 19.
[2] Long Shot

*See text for discussion of special situation.
+ 1 See text for discussion of special situation.

195

ber of new super league teams recommended by the interest-ability index. For New York, the result of the operation is 1.72; for Texas, 7.12; and for South Carolina, 2.00. Rounding these results, we have two teams allocated to New York, two to South Carolina, and seven to Texas.

The interest-ability index helps to refine the locational assignments based on population alone, but at least three other factors must be considered before final recommendations can be made. Attendance is an excellent measure of interest. In addition, we must examine tradition, or past success, and have a look at any special situations that might bear on the future success of an institution within a professional system (table 13).

Home-game attendance helps to pinpoint the entertainment value associated with any collegiate program. It also indicates the financial viability of the program. An average home attendance of 70,000 per contest tells us that the product being offered is truly fulfilling an entertainment need. Attendance of this magnitude means a great influx of money for the program and helps to insure the maintenance of a first-class team. Conversely an attendance average of 25,000 per game suggests that demand for the product is marginal and, in *most* cases, that the product is apt to be inferior.

Attendance is related to the availability of competitive entertainment and the level of local involvement with the game. At many schools it may vary by 25 percent or more from one season to the next. Winning seasons obviously inspire better attendance than losing ones. To eliminate the effects of a good or bad season I am taking each school's best average attendance figure from the past four years. This should provide an excellent measure of recent peak demand for the entertainment product.

The attendance figures are paced by the same group of schools that have dominated the national rankings (table 14). Michigan, Ohio State, Nebraska, Tennessee, Oklahoma, Michigan State,

Table 14: Win-Loss Records, 1952–83

	W	L	T	Per-cent		W	L	T	Per-cent
Oklahoma	259	69	7	.784	Ohio	164	150	7	.522
Ohio State	240	64	8	.782	Arizona	169	156	9	.519
Penn State	250	74	4	.768	Texas Tech	167	157	13	.515
Alabama	250	73	14	.763	Duke	164	156	14	.512
Texas	248	76	6	.761	Louisville	162	157	4	.508
Ariz. State	247	84	4	.743	Stanford	164	161	9	.504
USC	238	85	13	.728	Army	156	154	13	.503
Michigan	226	87	7	.717	Utah	167	166	3	.501
Nebraska	236	95	7	.709	S. Carolina	162	166	7	.494
Miami, Ohio	223	90	9	.707	Cincinnati	157	163	11	.491
Notre Dame	226	95	8	.699	San Jose	158	164	9	.491
Arkansas	227	100	5	.691	Minnesota	152	158	11	.491
Michigan	219	100	6	.683	SMU	158	165	11	.490
UCLA	216	100	14	.676	W. Michigan	149	156	9	.489
Auburn	216	107	8	.665	Toledo	154	162	7	.488
Mississippi	210	109	11	.653	Wisconsin	148	158	14	.484
Tennessee	212	110	14	.652	New Mexico	160	171	6	.484
S. Mississippi	211	113	6	.648	S.W. Louisiana	153	164	9	.483
San Diego	205	109	10	.648	N.C. State	154	168	11	.479
Georgia	210	113	13	.644	Temple	141	155	9	.477
Nevada-LV	109	61	3	.639	Baylor	153	171	9	.473
LSU	207	114	15	.638	Texas A & M	152	171	12	.472
Bowling Green	196	111	10	.634	Air Force	131	149	11	.469
Dartmouth	181	104	7	.632	N. Illinois	147	167	4	.469
Boston College	195	120	5	.617	Oklahoma State	149	172	12	.465
Yale	181	111	7	.617	Kent State	143	173	5	.453
Harvard	170	105	12	.613	Cornell	127	155	10	.452
Houston	196	123	11	.611	E. Michigan	129	160	13	.449
Florida	196	125	14	.606	Miss. State	141	175	12	.448
E. Carolina	193	125	7	.605	Pacific	144	179	7	.447
W. Virginia	193	132	7	.592	Iowa State	141	178	9	.444
Missouri	191	131	12	.590	Iowa	136	174	9	.440
Rutgers	185	129	3	.588	Oregon	140	181	14	.439
Michigan State	182	129	9	.583	California	142	184	9	.437
Clemson	187	135	11	.578	Kansas	138	180	15	.437
Ball State	170	123	9	.578	Kentucky	139	182	14	.436
Washington	188	137	8	.577	Illinois	132	177	11	.430

Table 14: Win-Loss Records, 1952–83 (*Continued*)

	W	L	T	Per-cent		W	L	T	Per-cent
Georgia Tech	188	137	11	.576	Fullerton	66	88	2	.429
Princeton	164	122	6	.572	N. Mex. State	138	185	7	.429
Wyoming	187	139	9	.572	Brown	114	167	9	.409
Virginia Tech	186	139	8	.571	Oregon State	131	194	6	.405
Fresno State	189	143	3	.569	Colorado State	132	200	6	.399
Maryland	186	142	5	.566	Wash. State	127	196	11	.397
Syracuse	180	138	4	.565	Wichita State	126	194	9	.397
Purdue	171	132	16	.561	Penn	109	175	8	.387
Pittsburgh	179	140	11	.559	TCU	121	198	15	.385
Long Beach	163	129	2	.558	Tulane	123	202	9	.382
Hawaii	178	141	5	.557	Vanderbilt	112	204	17	.362
Florida State	180	143	12	.555	Rice	115	208	10	.360
Utah State	183	146	8	.555	UTEP	114	211	8	.354
Colorado	179	145	9	.551	Indiana	108	207	5	.345
Memphis State	173	145	7	.543	Wake Forest	103	222	9	.322
N. Carolina	177	150	5	.541	Virginia	105	224	3	.321
Tulsa	178	152	4	.539	Northwestern	97	217	5	.312
Navy	169	146	13	.535	Kansas State	98	231	4	.300
Miami, Florida	174	152	5	.533	Columbia	77	206	9	.279
BYU	176	155	6	.531					

Missouri, Alabama, and LSU are in the top ten. Wisconsin and Tennessee are the only schools with consistently high attendance that have not met with as much recent success on the field. Just twenty-seven schools averaged over 50,000 fans per contest for the period 1973–83. Of these, all but Iowa, Illinois, Michigan State, Wisconsin, and Kentucky compiled winning records during the decade.

Another fourteen schools have attracted between 40,000 and 50,000 spectators per home game. Several of these—Arizona, Maryland, Arkansas, Oklahoma State, Texas A & M, Pittsburgh, and UCLA—either are among the nation's elite or are rapidly approaching that status.

Fifteen schools have averaged 30,000–40,000 fans per game

during the 1973–83 period. Recent national champions Miami and BYU were in that category, as were big winners Houston, SMU, and Maryland. In summary, fifty-seven schools were able to attract an average of 30,000 or more for eleven seasons between 1973 and 1983.

Based on the cost of running a big-time program and the average price of tickets, 30,000 per game is the absolute minimum required for super league status.[4] Although there may be a few exceptions, 40,000 per game would usually be necessary to break even.

TRADITION

One measure of a university's football tradition is their long-term winning percentage. There is strong evidence that consistent winning for a period of years promotes the chances for continued winning. Put simply, success breeds success.

The 1953–83 win-loss records of the current division IA schools are grouped into three winning percentage categories (figure 66). Just ten schools recorded a winning percentage of 70 percent or greater over the thirty-two-year span (table 14). Another seventeen won at least 60 percent of their games. Most of the programs, as would be expected, were mediocre. Thirteen schools, however, were perennial losers.

The national polls represent another measure of success and tradition. Though far from foolproof, the polls are a reasonable indicator of a team's relative ability. Goudge quantified the roll of the polls by totaling top-twenty appearances between 1952 and 1983. He utilized both the Associated Press (AP) and the United Press International (UPI) final results, awarding twenty points for a first-place finish, nineteen for second, on down to one point for twentieth place. By awarding points from both polls (number one in AP equals twenty points and number one in UPI equals twenty points, a total of forty points), he over-weighted higher finishes, thus reflecting the media and fan opinions regarding the prestige of Top Ten recognition.

The polls have been dominated by a select few (see chapter 5,

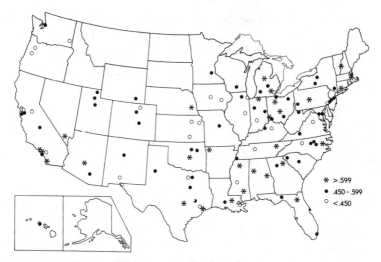

Figure 66. College football win-loss percentages, 1952–83.

table 3). Tradition is a function of consistency. Powers like Oklahoma, Alabama, Ohio State, Notre Dame, and Texas seldom have a really bad season. At the other extreme, Wake Forest, San Jose, and Kansas State have never recorded a Top Twenty finish.

Bowl appearances provide another indicator of an institution's tradition and recognition (table 15). The number of bowl games is highly correlated with winning percentage and poll values. In recent years, with the proliferation of postseason contests, average home-game attendance has become more significant as a selection factor. Home support generally translates into fan travel to the bowl site, thus providing schools with large attendance with another advantage over their small-crowd competitors.

A successful tradition is obviously a combination of factors. Winning percentage, poll recognition, bowl games, television appearances, All Americans, NFL alumni, coaching stability, and access to talent all play a part in its development. Using these variables Goudge categorized institutions into three groups (figure 67).[5] His tabular results demonstrate the major gaps that separate the top thirty-five schools from the pack (table 16). They have

Table 15: Bowl Game Appearances, 1952–83

	No.	W	L	T	Per-cent		No.	W	L	T	Per-cent
Alabama	27	16	10	1	0.611	Rice	4	1	3	0	0.250
Texas	24	11	12	1	0.479	S. Carolina	4	0	4	0	0.000
Nebraska	21	12	9	0	0.571	Toledo	4	4	0	0	1.000
Penn State	21	15	6	0	0.714	Tulane	4	1	3	0	0.250
Mississippi	19	10	9	0	0.526	Tulsa	4	1	3	0	0.250
LSU	18	9	9	0	0.500	California	3	0	3	0	0.000
Oklahoma	18	12	5	1	0.694	Duke	3	1	2	0	0.333
Arkansas	17	8	9	0	0.471	Kentucky	3	2	1	0	0.667
Ohio State	17	9	8	0	0.529	Michigan State	3	2	1	0	0.667
Florida	16	7	9	0	0.438	Minnesota	3	1	2	0	0.333
Tennessee	16	7	9	0	0.438	Virginia Tech	3	0	3	0	0.000
USC	16	11	5	0	0.688	Vanderbilt	3	2	1	0	0.667
Georgia Tech	15	9	6	0	0.600	Arizona	2	0	2	0	0.000
Georgia	15	6	9	0	0.400	Boston College	2	0	2	0	0.000
Auburn	14	7	7	0	0.500	Indiana	2	1	1	0	0.500
Missouri	13	8	5	0	0.615	Louisville	2	1	1	0	0.500
Michigan	12	3	9	0	0.250	N. Mex. State	2	2	0	0	1.000
N. Carolina	12	7	5	0	0.583	Ohio	2	0	2	0	0.000
Pittsburgh	12	6	6	0	0.500	Bowling Green	1	0	1	0	0.000
Texas Tech	12	2	10	0	0.167	Fresno State	1	1	0	0	1.000
Florida State	11	3	8	0	0.273	Fullerton	1	0	1	0	0.000
Maryland	11	3	8	0	0.273	Kansas State	1	0	1	0	0.000
Notre Dame	11	8	3	0	0.727	Kent State	1	0	1	0	0.000
West Virginia	11	6	5	0	0.545	New Mexico	1	1	0	0	1.000
Baylor	10	4	6	0	0.400	Pacific	1	1	0	0	1.000
UCLA	10	4	6	0	0.400	San Jose State	1	0	1	0	0.000
BYU	9	4	5	0	0.444	Utah	1	1	0	0	1.000
Colorado	9	4	5	0	0.444	Utah State	1	0	1	0	0.000
Houston	9	5	4	0	0.556	W. Michigan	1	0	1	0	0.000
N. C. State	9	6	3	0	0.667	Wake Forest	1	0	1	0	0.000
Washington	9	6	3	0	0.667	Wash. State	1	0	1	0	0.000
Arizona State	8	7	1	0	0.875	Wichita State	1	0	1	0	0.000
Clemson	8	3	5	0	0.375	Army	0	0	0	0	.
Oklahoma State	8	6	2	0	0.750	Ball State	0	0	0	0	.
Syracuse	8	3	5	0	0.375	C. Michigan	0	0	0	0	.
E. Carolina	7	5	2	0	0.714	Cincinnati	0	0	0	0	.
Stanford	7	6	1	0	0.857	Colorado State	0	0	0	0	.

Table 15: Bowl Game Appearances, 1952–83 *(continued)*

	No.	W	L	T	Per-cent		No.	W	L	T	Per-cent
Texas A & M	7	4	3	0	0.571	E. Michigan	0	0	0	0	.
Miami, Florida	6	3	3	0	0.500	Hawaii	0	0	0	0	.
SMU	6	3	3	0	0.500	Long Beach	0	0	0	0	.
S. Mississippi	6	1	5	0	0.167	Memphis State	0	0	0	0	.
Iowa	5	3	2	0	0.600	Nevada-LV	0	0	0	0	.
Miami, Ohio	5	3	2	0	0.600	Northwestern	0	0	0	0	.
Navy	5	3	2	0	0.600	Rutgers	0	0	0	0	.
TCU	5	1	3	1	0.300	S. W. Louisiana	0	0	0	0	.
UTEP	5	4	1	0	0.800	San Diego State	0	0	0	0	.
Wisconsin	5	2	3	0	0.400	Temple	0	0	0	0	.
Wyoming	5	3	2	0	0.600	Virginia	0	0	0	0	.
Air Force	4	1	2	1	0.375	Yale	0	0	0	0	.
Illinois	4	2	2	0	0.500	Brown	0	0	0	0	.
Iowa State	4	0	4	0	0.000	Columbia	0	0	0	0	.
Kansas	4	1	3	0	0.250	Cornell	0	0	0	0	.
Miss. State	4	3	1	0	0.750	Dartmouth	0	0	0	0	.
N. Illinois	4	2	2	0	0.500	Harvard	0	0	0	0	.
Oregon	4	2	2	0	0.500	Penn	0	0	0	0	.
Oregon State	4	2	2	0	0.500	Princeton	0	0	0	0	.
Purdue	4	4	0	0	1.000						

dominated in all categories of achievement. The middle group has had an occasional taste of the pie, while the lower third has been hopelessly chasing after the unattainable. During the most recent period, 1973–83, the gap has been widened, signifying an increasing domination by the most elite members of the Division IA club (table 17).

Tradition, combined with attendance and locational characteristics, is a significant factor in the decision to rate Wyoming and Syracuse as good bets. It is not enough, however, to warrant the inclusion of TCU, Rice, Oregon, Oregon State, or any of the Ivy League schools. The Southwest Conference schools have been away from the limelight too long and are severely constrained by

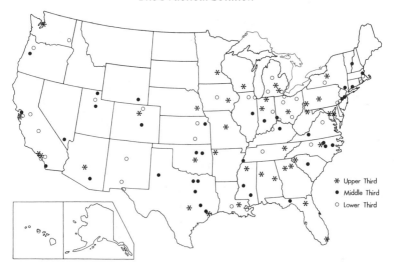

Figure 67. Composite success, 1952–83.

their proximity to NFL franchises. Ivy League members have made it clear that they want no part of big-time football as it is currently structured. As a consequence, their rich tradition has no bearing on the election process. Oregon and Oregon State have both experienced a degree of success in the past, but their presence in the same state reduces support for both programs. If attitudes and loyalties could be reshaped, then one of the programs would be a good bet.

SPECIAL SITUATIONS

There are several special situations that demand consideration prior to the final selection of the super league teams. Could the national service academies be accommodated? All students enrolled at the service academies are treated equally from a subsidy standpoint. The additional time requirements that would be imposed on the academy athletes might prove intolerable, though recent Air Force and Army teams have been nationally ranked despite devoting much less time to football than most of their com-

203

Table 16: Average Values of the Most Successful, Least Successful, and Middle-of-the-Road Programs

Success Variables
1952–83

Group	(Means)	Winning %*		Average Attendance*		Top Twenty*		National Television*		Regional Television*	
High	(1)	A	.603	A	47,223	A	271	A	13.8	A	21.5
Middle	(2)	B	.546	B	24,115	B	43	B	2.7	B	10.1
Low	(3)	C	.444	C	18,248	B	21	B	1.8	B	7.4

		Consensus All-Americans*		Conference Championships*		Bowl Trips*		Bowl W-L %*	
	(1)	A	12.1	A	5.33	A	11.4	A	.517
	(2)	B	1.7	B	3.13	B	3.7	B	.327
	(3)	B	.9	B	2.13	B	1.8	B A	.468

		Heisman*		Outland*		Undefeated Season*		National Championships*	
	(1)	A	.64	A	.69	A	1.31	A	.74
	(2)	B	.05	B	.08	B	.27	B	.05
	(3)	B	.08	B	.02	B	.24	B	.02

SOURCE: Theodore Goudge, 1984.

Table 17: Average Values by Time Periods of the Most Successful, Least Successful, and Middle-of-the-Road Programs

Group	(Means)				Success Variables Early 1952–61			

		Winning %		Average Attendance*		Top Twenty*	
High	(1)	A	.567	A	35,397	A	70.1
Middle	(2)	A	.533	B	18,474	B	22.3
Low	(3)	A	.507	B	15,483	B	14.3

Middle, 1962–72

		Winning %*		Average Attendance*		Top Twenty*	
	(1)	A	.589	A	45,703	A	90.2
	(2)	B A	.542	B	24,877	B	13.0
	(3)	B	.483	B	20,352	B	6.4

Late, 1973–83

		Winning %*		Average Attendance*		Top Twenty*	
	(1)	A	.646	A	57,519	A	110.7
	(2)	B	.555	B	27,751	B	8.1
	(3)	C	.356	C	19,088	B	0.3

SOURCE: Theodore Goudge, 1984.

petitors. Thus the academies are questionable candidates for super league status.

Rutgers represents another type of special situation. The major state university of New Jersey has been quietly moving up the football respectability ladder. Since 1972 Rutgers has begun to compete actively for the state's best football talent—talent plentiful enough to meet the needs of four to five major college teams. Rutgers is now committed to a big-time program. The move has been coordinated by the university's president, Edward Bloustein, and by alumnus Sonny Werblin, chairman of the New Jersey Sports and Exhibition Authority (Meadowlands Complex). In explanation of the current thrust, Werblin observed: "I noticed in traveling around that we had so many New Jersey boys playing on championship teams it was a shame we couldn't keep them home. If we could inculcate a *state pride* [italics added] in them we could have a great football team composed of boys from the state."[6] Bloustein defends the policy in terms of increased cultural benefits for the state: "Athletics identifies us as a state university in all aspects in everyone's mind. An athletic program is part of the legitimate cultural outlets of the people of the state, and I think this is a cultural as well as an educational institution for the State of New Jersey."[7]

Rutgers plans to use nearby Giants stadium for future games. The university is now scheduling eastern powers like Pittsburgh and Penn State and developing plans for intersectional games.

Wyoming—a reasonable tradition, national ranking in the 1960s, extremely loyal fans, and the state's only university—is another special situation. Attendance averages just 22,000 fans per game now, but with the recent growth spurt of the state's population there is potential for many more. Tulsa has also made the national rankings despite meager attendance. On the other hand, Northwestern, Oregon State, Oregon, Wake Forest, TCU, Rice, and New Mexico seem destined for purely amateur programs. All are plagued by varying combinations of poor location, disenchanted fans, suffocating competition from the pros, limited access to high school talent, and diminishing resources.

Final Selections

On the basis of the computer analysis, home-game attendance patterns, program tradition, the interest and ability index, and consideration of special situations, a total of forty-eight teams emerge as prime candidates for a collegiate super league (table 18). Another

Table 18: Prime Candidates and Good Bets

Air Force	Iowa State	Penn State
Alabama	Kansas	Pittsburgh
Arizona	Kentucky	Purdue
Arizona State	LSU	Rutgers
Arkansas	Maryland	SMU
Army	Miami, Florida	South Carolina
Auburn	Michigan	Stanford
Baylor	Michigan State	Syracuse
Boston College	Minnesota	Tennessee
BYU	Mississippi	Texas
California	Mississippi State	Texas A & M
Clemson	Missouri	Texas Tech
Colorado	Navy	UCLA
Florida	Nebraska	USC
Florida State	North Carolina	Virginia
Georgia	North Carolina State	Virginia Tech
Georgia Tech	Notre Dame	Washington
Houston	Ohio State	West Virginia
Illinois	Oklahoma	Wisconsin
Iowa	Oklahoma State	

dozen rate as good bets to survive within a super league format. In addition, I have identified fourteen long-shot contenders. Of the forty-eight sure bets only eleven are located in NFL cities. One of the urban teams, Pitt, was 1976 national champion, USC won in 1978 and Miami won in 1983; Houston is a SWC power; SMU, Boston College and UCLA are bona fide contenders; and Minnesota and Washington are the primary universities in their respective states, with strong traditions and good support by their fans.

Most of the prime candidates are situated in medium-sized communities far removed from the influence of professional football teams. Nebraska, Arkansas, Kentucky, Maryland, Missouri, Wisconsin, Minnesota, and Rutgers are the only major football universities in their respective states. Where the land grant tradition is strongest, primarily throughout the farm belt and the southeast, two equally strong state universities have frequently emerged. As

Table 19: Long Shots

Cincinnati	Miami, Ohio	Tulane
Duke	UNLV	Tulsa
Hawaii	Oregon	Utah
Indiana	San Diego State	Washington State
Louisville	San Jose State	Wyoming
Memphis State		

a result, several states have developed two schools equipped for superpower competition, e.g., Alabama–Auburn, Michigan–Michigan State, Iowa–Iowa State, Oklahoma–Oklahoma State, North Carolina–North Carolina State, and South Carolina–Clemson. Then there are football-crazy Texas, with at least five candidates for inclusion, and populous California, with great high school programs and its own array of traditional collegiate powers.

The long-shot group (table 19) is a combination of newcomers, second fiddlers, and the service academies. Half are independent and just two are affiliated with elite conferences. Most lack tradition and some have inadequate stadiums. Many would have to overcome long-term problems with more powerful competing state institutions.

The remainder of the Division IA membership would be well advised to concentrate on strictly amateur programs (table 20). This dropout group includes some members of major conferences who have known the taste of past glory. Many, however, have been fighting a losing battle for decades.

The foregoing selection process was for the present moment — the purpose was to choose a group of superpowers which could begin competition as soon as possible. Although it is based chiefly on population distribution and geographical differences in ability and interest, the roles of tradition and attendance have significantly influenced the final recommendations. What the analysis cannot take into account are the ramifications of the new environment which professionalization would create.

In a situation where everything is above board, where the job

Table 20: Dropouts

Arkansas State	Ohio
Ball State	Oregon State
Bowling Green	Pacific
Central Michigan	Rice
Colorado State	Southern Mississippi
Drake	Southwestern Louisiana
East Carolina	TCU
Eastern Michigan	Temple
Fresno State	Toledo
Fullerton State	Utah State
Kansas State	UTEP
Long Beach State	Vanderbilt
New Mexico	Wake Forest
NIU	Western Michigan
Northwestern	Wichita State

description fits the actual job, where athletes are being fairly compensated for services rendered, it is conceivable that some of the institutions which de-emphasized might see fit to climb aboard once again. Ivy League schools, possessed of excellent football traditions and a huge potential market, could be tempted. Even taking the NFL franchises into account, Pennsylvania, New York, and New England have very few teams relative to their population. Yale, Harvard, Penn, Columbia, Cornell, Brown, Princeton, and Dartmouth all have advantageous locations and ample financial resources.

Illinois, Ohio, and Michigan are also underrepresented in regard to both population and involvement with schoolboy football. Facilities are the immediate obstacle. Market potential exists for institutions like Bowling Green, Kent State, Western, Central, and Eastern Michigan, Illinois State, Northern Illinois, and Southern Illinois, though alumni support and tradition are feeble. The unanswerable question at present is whether or not positive market characteristics would eventually overcome the currently overriding negative forces.

A final factor to be considered is the matter of state pride. It has been a weighty ingredient in the evolution of the current geography of big-time intercollegiate football. State pride and spirit, together with a thirst for national attention, could prompt citizens in New Mexico, Oregon, Idaho, Montana, and the Dakotas to pool their resources and support teams. If this occurred, New Mexico and Oregon could each establish a franchise. In addition, a Dakota regional franchise and one combining Montana and Idaho might also be feasible. Each would require careful planning and a strong commitment from groups with widely divergent interests and purposes. They would be very difficult to develop, much less sustain.

It seems obvious that the new order would be in a state of flux for several years. But this is true of the present system. New challengers, like Houston, BYU, San Diego State, the Arizona and North Carolina schools, and Oklahoma State, have risen while old powers, including the service academies, Northwestern, TCU, and Syracuse, have fallen back.

The prime candidates, however, should all fare well, and some of the possibles could move up as others fade from view. Instability will be the norm among the long shots, and any one of the current dropouts might decide to come out of retirement. Under the new system, as under the old, there will be room for the outsiders and the long shots as well as for the dropouts.

12
Implementation
of the New System

A professional super-league system could solve many of the perplexing problems that now hamper intercollegiate athletics. We have already addressed the pressing need to eliminate the hypocrisy surrounding the student-athlete myth. An honest program, catering to the needs of both student and nonstudent pros, would be in keeping with the stated purposes of the American university. It would remove a serious obstacle to the attainment of the goals for which institutions of higher education were established. And, perhaps more important, it would demonstrate to all faculty and students that an environment of honesty and truth does indeed prevail.

There are many organizational alternatives for the new system. The following are my suggestions for its implementation. They apply to the recruitment of athletes and to the conditions of their eligibility, compensation, and matriculation to the major professional teams. I also have some recommendations in regard to the geographical structuring of competition and playoffs, the governance of amateur intercollegiate athletics, and the myriad of thorny questions involved in providing equal rights for women athletes.

Recruiting

The overriding concern of this book is athletic recruiting. It can, and most certainly should, be eliminated. Under the proposed system a draft of high school seniors, college and junior college players, supplemented by a summer free-agent trial period for those not drafted, would displace all recruiting. Schools could pool resources and set up scouting networks similar to those employed by professional football, basketball, and baseball organizations.

The frenzy of collegiate athletic recruiting is in stark contrast to the orderly player draft systems which have been established for professional sport. Player drafting was pioneered by the National Football League in an attempt to maintain a balance of power among league members. Teams drafted the top college seniors in reverse order of their finish in the league standing. Thus the worst teams were able to sign the best players and, at least theoretically, improve their competitive position. Active recruiting was replaced by scouting and a concentration on strategies for ferreting out the best prospects.

Professional basketball emulated the NFL and established a draft system of its own. Early versions of the draft contained a territorial component, allowing teams first rights to a player from their designated territory. Professional baseball finally embraced the drafting concept in 1965. The draft has functioned well for professional sport and it should also function efficiently for the collegiate super league.

I would prefer to see the draft organized along regional lines. Draft regions would be drawn up in a manner similar to that described in chapter 10. A regional drafting scheme would produce teams composed primarily of players from their own locale; they would be truly representative of their home areas and would retain their regional identity. Intersectional contests would be just that, with players from one section of the country pitted against those from another.

Regional drafting could foster imbalances in the power structure. Teams situated in areas with an abundance of high school talent might grow to dominate those from less favored locales. If this occurred, the recruiting territories of the disadvantaged would have to be expanded.

The draft would operate as follows. Assuming that competition would commence with approximately sixty teams of 50–60 players each, total league manpower requirements would range between 3,000 and 3,600. A five-year eligibility period for high school draftees and a three-year term for those drafted from the junior colleges seem reasonable. Allowing for attrition due to injury and for other sorts of dropouts, as well as for early matriculation to the NFL, there would probably be an annual need for 1,000 to 1,100 new players. During the break-in period, players currently at the major colleges would be eligible during the initial draft. Those not selected would be carried on scholarship through their senior year.

After the break-in phase the draft would likely stabilize at an annual level of twenty-five new players per team. After a two- or three-week summer camp for draftees and "free agents,"[1] rosters would be trimmed so as to include an average of twenty new players per team. Rules could be established to let the figure vary between fifteen and twenty-five per team, depending on the number of holdovers at each institution.

I believe that the NFL should be able to draft a player from the collegiate professional league at any time after his third year of competition. Some would be ready sooner, but for the sake of stability, a three-year waiting period is reasonable. Most would probably compete four or five years, moving up or out at the conclusion of that time span. Once signed, a player would be guaranteed access to a free education regardless of how long he played. The responsibility for pursuing an education, however, would be solely his. James Michener, in his *Sports in America,* also suggests a professional setup for college football and basketball.[2] Michener's plan allows an athlete to enroll in one course during the season, a full load during the off season, and summer school. It also guarantees a fifth year (tuition and board free) to complete degree requirements. Michener goes on to recommend that free tuition should remain in effect for a period of fourteen years after departure from college, thereby encouraging degree work for those athletes who continue playing at a higher professional level.

Although the proposed system of professional collegiate franchises is fair to the vast majority of athletes, it does discriminate against those possessing legitimate scholarly ambitions and abilities. There is a small minority of academically gifted athletes. For those, I recommend a flexible program that would allow enrollment in some coursework during the athletic season. By taking advantage of that option as well as carrying a full academic load during off-season terms, the majority could complete their degrees while in residence. For those who desire to specialize in pursuits available at only a select group of schools, I would recommend freedom of choice. The academically gifted (those scoring in the 90th percentile or above on nationally standardized college aptitude examinations) could bypass the draft and select the school that best met their needs.

What happens to all the talented players who are not quite good enough for the super league? Ideally, they would be able to compete at one of the 400 to 500 colleges or junior colleges which would still be sponsoring amateur football. There would be no athletic scholarships and no recruiting. Athletes desiring a college education would enroll as students and pursue sport strictly as a recreational extracurricular activity. Off-season practice would not be allowed, coaches would have no more control of the student-athlete's life than that exerted by any of the other faculty members. Violators of a greatly simplified amateur athletic code would be severely disciplined. For example, coaches found guilty of infractions after a fair trial would be banned from coaching for five to ten years. The athletes involved would be prohibited from all further collegiate competition.

Pay Scale

I favor a standardized pay scale for all members of the super league. The details would have to be resolved by representatives of the sponsoring institutions and the players. Compensation should be scaled so that costs and expenses would be approximately equal for the middle range of the league membership. Player salaries should be geared to anticipated revenues of schools like Iowa State, Mississippi, and Texas Tech, rather than to those of Michigan, Notre Dame, or Penn State. Adaptation to the middle range of gross income would produce salary levels something like this:

> 1st year players — $15,000
> 2nd year players — $17,500
> 3rd year players — $20,000
> 4th year players — $22,500
> 5th year players — $25,000

All of the prime candidates could live comfortably with an initial salary schedule of this magnitude. Some of the other possibilities, however, would have difficulty meeting the payroll.

A second-tier collegiate professional league with a salary schedule proportionate to expected revenues is another alternative. In fact, after a few years of operation, it is probable that the super league would be split into two divisions. Division A, comprising the prime candidates, would pay higher salaries and would field teams a cut above those of Division B, a group that would include a few of the prime candidates, the long shots, and any newcomers who decide to opt for the professional ranks.

Basketball could be operated in much the same fashion. As many as 250 schools would draft a total of nearly 1,800 players each year.

Table 21: Conference Alignment and Membership

Atlantic	Pacific	Northern	Mid West
Boston College	Arizona	Air Force	Illinois
Clemson	Arizona State	BYU	Iowa
Maryland	California	Colorado	Iowa State
Navy	Stanford	Kansas	Notre Dame
North Carolina	UCLA	Minnesota	Purdue
North Carolina State	USC	Nebraska	Wisconsin
South Carolina	Washington		
Virginia			
Virginia Tech			

Mid East	Mid South	Deep South	Tex OK
Army	Arkansas	Alabama	Baylor
Michigan	Kentucky	Auburn	Houston
Michigan State	LSU	Florida	Oklahoma
Ohio State	Mississippi	Florida State	Oklahoma State
Penn State	Mississippi State	Georgia	SMU
Pittsburgh	Missouri	Georgia Tech	Texas
Rutgers	Tennessee	Miami, Florida	Texas A & M
Syracuse			Texas Tech
West Virginia			

Conferences and Playoffs

I propose that the super league commence operations with an eight-conference format composed of fifty-nine teams. I have assembled the conferences so that they represent, as accurately as possible, distinct geographic regions (table 21). They have been set up to preserve traditional rivalries; for example, Michigan–Ohio State, Oklahoma–Texas, Notre Dame–Purdue, UCLA–USC, and Clemson–South Carolina. In addition, the conferences have been designed to build new confrontations which make sense geographically but, which for various reasons, have never developed. Included are Arkansas–LSU and Missouri, Penn State– Ohio State and Michigan, Missouri–Kentucky, Iowa–Iowa State, Maryland–Rutgers and Nebraska–Wisconsin and Minnesota.[3]

Assuming a fourteen-game season, scheduling could either follow a round-robin system, with each conference member playing all other conference members twice, or could combine one round of conference competition with variety of interconference matchups. A few years of experimentation would undoubtedly produce the most feasible alternative.

The playoff system for the national championship would look something like this:

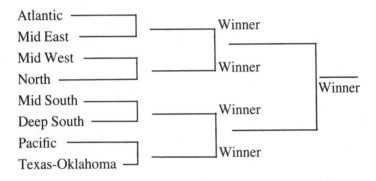

Atlantic
Mid East
Mid West
North
Mid South
Deep South
Pacific
Texas-Oklahoma

Winner
Winner
Winner
Winner
Winner

Six of the seven major bowls would serve as the quarterfinal and semifinal playoff sites. On an alternating basis, the seventh bowl would host the championship game. Should greater postseason excitement be required, wild-card playoff teams selected on the merit of their season's record could be added. Sixteen teams would permit eight more bowl games while prolonging the season for only one week.

The playoffs would give the bowls more meaning, and, better yet, the mythical national champion would be replaced by the real McCoy.

Other Sports

The demand for other sports might similarly warrant the establishment of collegiate professional leagues. A wrestling is a case in point; at present there are at least twenty college programs that draw sufficient fan support—programs that come close to paying their own way. A wrestling league could be formed, and collegiate wrestling is set up in such a way that only token alterations to the existing tournament structure would be necessary.

On another front, those colleges with big-time baseball programs could openly acknowledge the fact that they are, in reality, a part of the minor league system. In so doing they might be able to obtain partial support from the major leagues. Collegiate baseball certainly deserves support from Major League teams, since they are the chief benefactors of the programs. It is conceivable that affiliations could be established between individual big league clubs and individual colleges thus bringing the colleges into the organized farm system. Collegiate hockey could be organized similarly, as it too serves in part as a training ground for the professional ranks.

One drawback to open professionalism for wrestling, track and field, or soccer would be the effect on eligibility for international and Olympic competition. Until a more realistic international amateur code can be written, it is doubtful that the Olympic sports could be accommodated within the projected system, despite the fact that under-the-table payments to "amateur" track and field performers are among the biggest in the world of sport.

There is no conceivable justification for universities' providing athletic scholarships for golf, tennis, gymnastics, swimming, or lacrosse. As things now stand, some universities are sponsoring subsidized training facilities for professional tennis, the PGA, and similar outlets. Ninety-nine percent of the students and faculty accrue no benefits from golf or tennis programs. The only winners are the golfers, the tennis players, and the professional associations. They are the ones who should foot the bill if there are to be subsidized golf and tennis programs in the colleges and universities.

Title IX—HEW Interpretations

The recent HEW interpretation of the Title IX legislation—equal rights for women athletes—makes the super league alternative even more appealing. Professionalize football, basketball, and any other sport (men's or women's) which can sustain itself, and eliminate aid to athletes in all other sports. Provide equal funds for intercollegiate athletic activities for men and women from the *educational* budget and from the school's share of the profits which result from the professional operations.

Unfortunately, women's athletic programs have rushed into the athletic scholarship business, undertaking the intensive recruiting and big-time promotions that will ultimately tie the athlete to the athletic department. In the name of equal rights, women's sports are emulating men's, much to the detriment of the athletes' academic development. It's the wrong road, but they are speeding down it nevertheless, in the name of equality.

It does not have to be that way. Now is the time to get things in perspective. We can have an honest system, one that fulfills the public craving for quality entertainment while serving legitimate student needs for extracurricular athletic activity.

Intercollegiate athletics are at a crossroads, as they were in the 1920s. The decision on which direction to take has been complicated by the rise of a strong new movement in sports—women are finally demanding and beginning to receive equal treatment. In so doing, they have helped us to understand what is wrong. The time for a new system is now, but first we must shed the influence of the old order, of those who promote and govern intercollegiate sport.

Notes

CHAPTER 1

1. Taken from an interview with Jerry Pettibone, former recruiting coordinator at the University of Oklahoma. Pettibone is currently on the football staff at the University of Nebraska.

2. Joseph Durso, *The Sports Factory* (New York: Quadrangle, 1975), pp. 3–7.

3. Ibid., p. 6.

4. *New York Times,* 12 March 1974, p. 42.

5. See Ken Denlinger and Leonard Shapiro, *Athletes for Sale* (New York: T. Y. Crowell, 1975).

6. Dan Jenkins, "Pursuit of a Big Blue Chipper," *Sports Illustrated,* 9 September 1968, pp. 104–24.

7. Ibid.

8. *New York Times,* 28 April 1974, p. 2.

9. Jim Benagh, *Making It to #1* (New York: Dodd, Mead and Co., 1976).

10. Durso, *Sports Factory,* pp. 31–46.

11. Ibid.

12. Benagh, *Making It,* pp. 31–53.

13. Ibid., p. 36.

14. Ibid., p. 47.

15. Willie Morris, *The Courting of Marcus Dupree* (New York, Doubleday, 1983).

16. Durso, *Sports Factory,* p. 114.

CHAPTER 2

1. David T. Voight's *American Baseball* (Norman, Oklahoma: University of Oklahoma Press, 1968) provides an in-depth examination of the early development of baseball. Voight also discusses the glory-of-the-town motivation relative to the growth of professionalism.

2. Albert B. Hart, "Status of Athletic Sports in American Colleges," *Atlantic Monthly,* July 1890, pp. 63–71.

3. For an extensive study of the role of boosters in the development of the United States see Daniel J. Boorstin, *The Americans: The Democratic Experience* (New York: Random House, 1973).

4. *Rockford* (Illinois) *Register,* 27 July 1867.

5. Howard J. Savage, *American College Athletics* (New York: The Carnegie Foundation for the Advancement of Teaching, 1929).

6. According to George Huff, the introduction of athletic training tables marked the beginning of professionalization. Occurring in the early 1900s, the programmed feeding operations put the whole team on the payroll. Taken from Jim Benagh, *Making It to #1* (New York: Dodd, Mead and Co., 1976), p. 197.

7. Allison Danzig, *Oh, How They Played the Game* (New York: Macmillan Co., 1971), pp. 324–28.

8. For example, see W. P. Bowen, "Evaluation of Athletic Evils," *American Physical Education Review,* XIV (March 1909), 151–56; L. B. R. Briggs, "Intercollegiate Athletics and War," *Atlantic Monthly,* September 1918, 304–309; William H. P. Faunce, "Character in Athletics," *National Education Association Proceedings,* 43 (1904), 558–64. Alexander Meiklejohn, "What Are College Games For?" *Atlantic Monthly,* November 1922, 663–71. Robert K. Root, "Sport vs. Athletics," *Forum,* 72 (November 1924), 657–64.

9. Savage, *College Athletics,* p. 225.

10. Ibid., p. 265.

11. *New York Times,* 31 March 1937, p. 16.

12. John R. Betts, *America's Sporting Heritage: 1850–1950* (Reading, Mass.: Addison Wesley, 1974), p. 350. Also see Robert M. Hutchins, *The Higher Learning in America* (New Haven: Yale University Press, 1936), p. 11 and "Gate Receipts and Glory," *Saturday Evening Post,* 211 (December 3, 1938): 23.

13. *New York Times,* 4 December 1947, p. 47.

14. *New York Times,* 19 May 1948, p. 38. Faurot did cite an agreement with

Kansas proclaiming Kansas City as "open territory," so long as there were no forays into St. Louis.

15. *New York Times*, 4 January 1952, p. 25.

16. Herman Hickman, "The College Football Crisis," *Sports Illustrated* 5 (6, 13 August, 1956): 6.

17. *New York Times*, 28 March 1951, p. 22.

CHAPTER 3

✓ 1. *Manual of the National Collegiate Athletic Association, 1984–85* (Shawnee Mission, Kansas: NCAA, 1985).

2. Robert Vare, *Buckeye* (New York: Harper's Magazine Press, 1974).

3. Ibid., pp. 78–79.

4. *Official Handbook of the National Federation of High School Athletic Associations* (Chicago: National Federation of High School Athletic Associations, 1983).

5. Vare, *Buckeye*, p. 81.

6. Ibid., p. 82.

7. Ibid., p. 84.

CHAPTER 4

1. Oklahoma A & M (now Oklahoma State University) had excellent teams during 1944 and 1945 but soon fell back to its former status.

2. For an account of the slush fund accusations see Douglas S. Looney, "Deep in Hot Water in Stillwater," *Sports Illustrated*, 3 July 1978, pp. 18–23.

CHAPTER 5

1. Darrell Crase, "Inner Circles of Football," *Athletic Administration* 7 (1972): 29.

2. For a detailed analysis of the origins of American football players during the 1960s, see John F. Rooney, Jr., *A Geography of American Sport* (Reading, Mass.: Addison Wesley, 1974).

3. Theodore L. Goudge, "A Geographical Analysis of Major College Football Programs: the Parameters of Success 1952–1953," Ed.D. diss., Oklahoma State University, 1984.

4. The 1971–72 sample is not perfectly comparable to the 1976–77 and 1980–81 samples. The earlier sample contains 180 schools (including several of the southern black institutions) and 11,786 football players. The later samples number 129 (including NCAA Division IA institutions, plus the seven Yankee

Conference schools) and accounts for 20,478 football players. The 1971–72 basketball sample includes 220 universities and 3,089 players, whereas the 1976–77 and 1980–81 data are based on 240 universities and 6,420 players. Where applicable, I have introduced my 1961–67 sample, which included 136 football rosters and 14,500 players as well as 161 basketball rosters and 4,200 players.

5. That legend is set forth eloquently by Michael Novak in *The Joy of Sports* (New York: Basic Books, 1976), p. 286: "The very words Notre Dame mean a certain kind of spirit: a spirit of never quitting, of using one's wit, of playing with desperate seriousness and intense delight, of achieving not just excellence but a certain kind of flair that must be thought of as a gift and grace. You can't think of Notre Dame without invoking a world in which grace and the miraculous are as linked to human excellence as atmosphere to earth."

CHAPTER 6

1. William Sutton, "An Analysis of Blue Chip Recruiting," Ed.D. diss., Oklahoma State University, 1982.

CHAPTER 7

1. Professor Turner utilized the 1977 NFL rosters. He gathered data on both the high school and collegiate backgrounds of NFL players.

CHAPTER 8

1. For a detailed study of basketball recruiting, see John F. Rooney, Jr., *A Geography of American Sport* (Reading, Mass.: Addison Wesley, 1974), and Roger L. Jenkinson, "The Geography of Indiana Interscholastic and Intercollegiate Basketball," (Ph.D. diss., Oklahoma State University, 1974).

2. Correspondence from Al Harden, April 1970.

3. Correspondence from Shelbyville, Indiana, basketball coach, April 1970.

4. Correspondence from Bill Chesbrough, athletic Director and head basketball coach at Elgin High School, Elgin, Illinois, April 1970.

5. For a description of the City Game, see Pete Axthelm, *The City Game* (New York: Harper & Row, 1970), and Rick Telander, *Heaven Is a Playground* (New York: St. Martin's Press, 1976).

CHAPTER 9

1. Bob Hurt, "How Do You Curb Cheats, Coaches?" *Daily Oklahoman*, 30 December 1976.

2. Doug Tucker, "Byers: 30% of Colleges Break Rules," *Tulsa World*, 26 August 1984.

3. *Austin American-Statesman*, 15 December 1976.

4. Jim Benagh, *Making It to #1* (New York: Dodd, Mead and Co., 1976), pp. 75–76.

5. George H. Hanford, *A National Study of Intercollegiate Athletics* (Washington, D.C.: American Council on Education, 1974), pp. 74–75.

6. Ibid.

7. Herman Hickman, "The College Football Crisis: Part I: To Bring Football Back to Its Rightful Place," *Sports Illustrated*, 6 August 1956, pp. 6–61.

8. Hurt, "How Do You Curb Cheats, Coaches?"

9. Murray Olderman, "Minuses Outweigh Pluses," *Newspaper Enterprise Association*, 26 December 1976.

10. Ibid.

CHAPTER 10

1. John Underwood, "Tell You What To Do," *Sports Illustrated*, 6 September 1976, pp. 26–30.

2. James Michener, *Sports in America* (New York: Random House, 1976), p. 223.

3. *New York Times*, 29 October 1951, p. 17.

4. Ibid.

5. George Plimpton, "But the Ivies Do Fight Fiercely," *Sports Illustrated*, 8 September 1975, pp. 29–39.

CHAPTER 11

1. This is by no means a new idea. See John R. Tunis, "More Pay for College Football Stars," *American Mercury*, November 1936, pp. 267–72. Tunis challenged the colleges to abandon their hypocritical attitudes toward amateur athletes and to pay the players openly. President John W. Taylor of the University of Louisville reiterated the proposal in 1947, calling for colleges to hire full-time pro teams to represent them: "No question of simon-pure amateurism would bother the schools which might take up the plan since the football players would not be students of the schools they represent. They would be hired just like professors" (*New York Times*, 8 September 1947, p. 27). Harold W. Stoke said much the same seven years later, in his "College Athletics: Education or Show Business," *Atlantic Monthly*, March 1954, pp. 46–50. Stoke urged colleges to accept athletics as entertainment, as business, and to shape the rules to reflect that reality.

2. Gary Smith, "Hello Trouble, I'm Dale Brown," *Sports Illustrated*, 18 November 1985, p. 45.

3. Based on private conversations during October 1976 and February 1977.

4. For six home games, 30,000 spectators, paying an average of $12.00 per ticket, would produce gross gate receipts of $2,160,000. Allowing for additional television and play-off revenue, income would be adequate to meet a fifty-player payroll of $15,000 per player ($750,000), as well as to pay the coaching staff and to cover normal operating expenses.

5. Goudge, "Geographical Analysis of Major College Football Programs.

6. Gordon S. White, Jr., "Rutgers Quietly and Smoothly Entering Big-Time Sports Era," *New York Times*, 11 November 1976, pp. 55–56.

7. Ibid.

CHAPTER 12

1. By the term free agent, I refer to any athlete who, after registering for the draft, failed to be selected by one of the super league teams. All players wishing to qualify for the super league would be required to register for the preseason draft. A player could not avoid the draft and then report to the team of his choice as a free agent.

2. James Michener, *Sports in America* (New York: Random House, 1976), pp. 200–203.

3. Iowa and Iowa State resumed football competition in 1977.

Index

227